LOOKING GOOD
ON THE WEB

Daniel Gray

CORIOLIS

The Coriolis Group, LLC
14455 N. Hayden Road, Suite 220
Scottsdale, Arizona 85260

480/483-0192
FAX 480/483-0193
http://www.coriolis.com

Library of Congress Cataloging-In-Publication Data
Gray, Daniel, 1961-
Looking good on the Web / by Daniel Gray.
p. cm
Includes index.
ISBN 1-57610-508-3
1. Web sites--Design. I. Title.
TK5105.888.G718 1999
005.7'2--DC21   99-43076
                                   CIP

Printed in the United States of America
10 9 8 7 6 5 4 3 2 1

President, CEO
Keith Weiskamp

Publisher
Steve Sayre

Acquisitions Editor
Mariann Hansen Barsolo

Marketing Specialist
Beth Kohler

Project Editor
Don Eamon

Technical Reviewer
John Shanley and Brian Little

Production Coordinator
Meg E. Turecek

Cover Design
Jody Winkler
additional art provided by Brandon Riza

Layout Design
April Nielsen

Other Titles For The Creative Professional

3D Studio MAX R3 f/x and design
by Jon A. Bell

3D Studio MAX R3 In Depth
by Rob Polevoi

Adobe ImageStyler In Depth
by Daniel Gray

After Effects 4 In Depth
by R. Shamms Mortier

Bryce 4 f/x and design
by R. Shamms Mortier

CorelDRAW 9 f/x and design
by Shane Hunt

Flash 4 Web Animation f/x and design
by Ken Milburn and John Croteau

Illustrator 8 f/x and design
by Sherry London and T. Michael Clark

Looking Good In Print, Fourth Edition
by Roger C. Parker

Looking Good In Presentations, Third Edition
by Molly Joss

Photoshop 5 Filters f/x and design
by T. Michael Clark

Photoshop 5 In Depth
by David Xenakis and Sherry London

To Debbie, Allie, and Colton.
—Daniel Gray

ABOUT THE AUTHOR

Daniel Gray is the author of *Adobe PageMill 3 f/x and design*, *Adobe ImageStyler In Depth*, *The Photoshop Plug-ins Book*, and a host of other books about graphics and Internet-related topics. Dan has spent his entire career in the graphics trenches, working on the Web since 1995 and writing computer books and articles since 1990. You can find his Web sites at **www.geekbooks.com** and **www.pluginbook.com**.

Acknowledgments

Looking Good On The Web is a distillation of the most frequently asked questions I've encountered over my Web design years. It's been an amazing trip. Web years are worse than dog years, in some respects—each with the potential of infinity, rather than a simple seven.

This book would not have been possible without the hard work and dedication of a wonderful team of people at The Coriolis Group. My heartfelt thanks to: Don Eamon for his expertise, patience, and extra mile at the project editing helm (including his masterful work with the Glossary); Mariann Barsolo for signing the book and her guidance in developing the concept; Chuck Hutchinson for a thorough, yet kind copyedit; John Shanley and Brian Little for their excellent technical editing and reviews; Meg Turecek for her precise layout; Jody Winkler, for a great cover; and April Nielsen, ace designer of the color section.

I can only hope you come away from this book with the right perspective. It's intended to help ease your entry into the world of Web design by encouraging the creation of great little Web sites. I wholeheartedly believe in designing simple, effective sites, where functionality is the name of the game. Fancy gadgets and gratuitous eye candy shouldn't waylay the budding designer.

Now go out there and design an awesome site!

dan@geekbooks.com
Somewhere in the Swamps of Joisey

Cheers,

—Daniel Gray

Contents At A Glance

TABLE OF CONTENTS

Chapter 4
Color On The Web

Chapter 5
Getting Started With Graphics

INTRODUCTION

What Does It Take To Look Good On The Web?

If you're new to Web design, the field can seem overwhelming. There are thousands of sources screaming to get your attention—from the software developers that want to sell you the latest whizbang program, to the 90-day-wonder in the MIS department who's become the resident expert on everything Web-related. It can be hard to get your bearings above the din. This book was written to help cut through the clutter, so that you can chart your course with purpose and clarity.

In working and corresponding with neophyte Webbies over the past five years, I've come to a conclusion. When it comes to Web design, it's always better to learn how to walk before you run. Solidly designed Web sites don't have to rely upon the latest bells and whistles. It's easy to fall victim to the siren song, but you need to steer clear, and keep your designs clean and simple. Great, high-traffic Web sites don't need to be cutting-edge examples of technology.

Who Needs This Book

Looking Good On The Web is intended for novice to intermediate Web page builders. It's designed to quickly acclimate new users, and to heighten the design sense of folks with some Web page building experience. The potential audience for this book includes:

- Business owners

- Graphic designers

- Marketing communications professionals

- Technical documentation specialists

- Non-profit organizations

- Budding entrepreneurs

- Educators

- Students

If you're well on your way as a high-end Web designer, this book *isn't* for you. If, however, you want—or need—information that will help start you out properly on that high-end road, this book *is* for you.

What's In The Book?

Looking Good On The Web was designed to ease you into the world of Web design. It's not a dry HTML guide, nor is it an esoteric design exercise. The book is divided into 12 common-sense chapters and an appendix. Here's a brief description of the elements:

- *Chapter 1, "Laying The Groundwork"*—This chapter helps you to answer a series of important questions before you begin building your Web site. When you fully understand the purpose of the site and the need of its visitors, you can define a goal, and refine your message.

- *Chapter 2, "Type On The Web"*—It's an imperfect world! This chapter covers the subject of typography on the Web, as it explains the limitations of legacy HTML and presents a range of alternatives—from the low-end through the high-end.

- *Chapter 3, "Building Forms"*—Forms are an important component of Web interactivity. This chapter explains how forms work, as it lays out each form element along with an overview of CGI scripts. You'll learn how to design clean and effective forms.

- *Chapter 4, "Color On The Web"*—This full-color chapter dives into the subject of color on the Web, as it explains the restrictions imposed by the browsers and platforms. You'll learn about topics including color depth, monitor gamma, dithering, and the 216-color Web palette.

- *Chapter 5, "Getting Started With Graphics"*—This chapter explains the various kinds of graphics and their uses in Web page design. You'll learn how to choose the proper file format (GIF or JPEG) and how to best compress your images for speedy downloads and flawless display.

- *Chapter 6, "Page Layout Basics"*—This chapter provides a fresh sheet of graph paper to enable you to build a solid page structure that best accommodates your audience. You'll learn about multiple column layouts, frames, and background images.

- *Chapter 7, "Navigational Systems"*—If you want your visitors to find what they need on your Web site, you need to provide the tools for them to do so. This chapter helps you choose a navigational orientation, and design the most effective interface.

- *Chapter 8, "Creating Site Structure"*—Are you going to build a cabin, a mansion, or a palace? This chapter enables you to envision your site structure, and craft a warm, effective design.

- *Chapter 9, "Adding Interactivity"*—Looking for the flash and sizzle? This chapter outlines the methods you can use to add interactivity to your site. It provides an overview of technologies including GIF animation, JavaScript, DHTML, Java, Shockwave, Audio, and Video.

- *Chapter 10, "Designing Web Advertising"*—Need to get the word out? This chapter explains the most common forms of Web advertising. You'll learn about the most common ad types and practices as you set your goals and build effective banner advertisements.

- *Chapter 11, "Conquering Design Problems"*—So that's why it doesn't work! You may find this chapter to be vital during your first eleventh-hour crisis situation. This chapter presents twenty ways to sink your ship (and the methods you can use to float it again). Use this chapter and learn from our mistakes.

- *Chapter 12, "Redesign Time"*—After your Web site comes online, you'll soon find yourself rethinking the design. This chapter helps you to approach the redesign process with confidence. You'll learn to design with flexibility in mind, as you make the crucial decisions on where to prune and expand, and you'll see why it's important to prevent your pages from "going 404".

- *Appendix, "Resources"*—This handy group of listings of Web site design resources should keep you clicking away happily for hours on end. You'll find a wide array of graphics, Java, JavaScript, CGI, and other great resource sites.

- *Glossary*—Sling the lingo like a pro! Flip to these pages to decipher those pesky Web buzz words.

Moving On

What does it take to look good on the Web? It isn't a walk in the park. Great Web sites take planning, perseverance, patience, and a lot of hard work. Too many times, I've seen novice Web designers who have bit off more than they could chew. In the valiant attempt to create a cool site, they lost sight of the true purpose. Don't make this mistake. Don't get hung up on the bells and whistles. Form follows function.

PS: don't forget to drop by my Web site, **geekbooks.com**, for updates and goodies.

PART I

THE BASICS OF WEB DESIGN

LAYING THE GROUNDWORK

1

Do your research, plan carefully, and get your Web site started on a solid foundation.

A contractor would not build a house without blueprints. Likewise, you should not embark upon a Web site project without a clean set of plans. Before you break ground on a new Web site, it's essential to have a clear understanding of the site's purpose. Making a major change in direction can be costly and difficult after development is underway.

At this stage of the project, you should find yourself in the role of the architect. This first chapter helps you ascertain purpose, define intent, and assess needs—before committing a single pixel to screen. The design and technical aspects come in subsequent chapters.

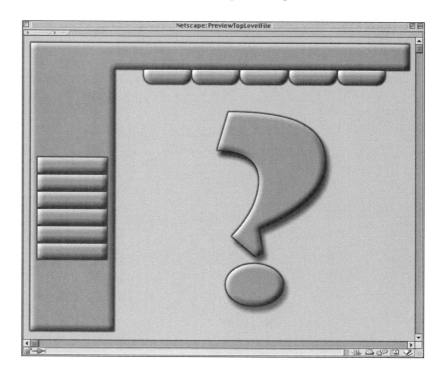

What Do You Have To Say?

Someone came up with the bright idea to build a Web site. "We have to have a Web presence!" Now, it's your responsibility to get the project underway. Before the first pixel is committed to the screen, you have to know what your site is going to say. A good architect takes the time to sit down with a client to understand his or her needs, desires, and expectations. Determining the proper course might take a series of meetings.

Understand Your Purpose

Why will the Web site exist? Begin by defining the overall mission and intent of the site. Don't get into specifics yet. Step back and look at the big picture. Then, ask yourself the most obvious questions.

Consider all of the following possibilities:

- *Small business*—Do you need to publicize a small business? What kinds of products and services does the small business provide? Who are the customers?

- *Educational*—Will the site exist for purely educational reasons? Will you be serving students, parents, alumni, or faculty?

- *Corporate*—Do you need to promote an established corporate entity? What divisions will require the most presence?

- *eCommerce*—Are you planning on selling a product online? Do you have the infrastructure—capability to accept credit cards, shipping and fulfillment, ongoing sales support—to support these sales?

- *Nonprofit organization*—Will the site carry the torch for a charity or other nonprofit entity? Do you want the site to reach out more to members or potential members?

- *Governmental*—Will the site support a governing body or organization?

- *Community*—Do you plan on creating an online community?

- *Personal*—Are you building the site just for fun or personal satisfaction, or do you have a message that the world needs to hear?

What kind of lot will your Web home sit upon? What kind of face will it show to the street? Think about the overall impression it will give to your visitors.

Define The General Goal

What does your organization need from the site? Define the general results you want to achieve. The following list will help you define your goals:

- *Small business*—The site needs to sell my wares. The site needs to attract sales leads.

- *Educational*—The site needs to inform.

- *Corporate*—The site needs to inform the (current and potential) investors. The site needs to inform the press. The site needs to support my customers.

- *eCommerce*—The site needs to sell product.

- *Nonprofit organization*—The site needs to raise money. The site needs to inform my patrons.

- *Governmental*—The site needs to inform my constituents.

- *Community*—The site needs to provide a means of communication.

- *Personal*—The site needs to tell my story.

When your visitors stroll up the walk to your doors, what will they find?

Nail Down The Methods

Now, let's get a little more specific. What methods can you use to meet these goals?

- *Small business*—Create a form to capture sales leads. Provide details on goods and services.

- *Educational*—Provide course catalogs, class schedules, and book requirements.

- *Corporate*—Post investor information, such as annual and quarterly reports. Post press releases. Provide details on products and services. Deliver online customer support.

- *eCommerce*—Create an online catalog with secure transactions.

- *Nonprofit organization*—Use a secure Web page to accept donations via credit card. Post news and information.

- *Governmental*—Post news and information. Give details on laws and regulations.

- *Community*—Provide features such as bulletin boards, chat rooms, and personal Web pages.

- *Personal*—Tell your story.

The goals and methods will determine the different rooms and pathways through your online home. Your visitors may want to get to the dining room, but they might find something of interest as they come in through the foyer or the kitchen. Over time, the traffic will leave wear marks in the carpet. You might find that the path from the back door is more popular than the path from the front door.

What Are Your Visitors Looking For?

Before a site is built, you must do your best to anticipate what your visitors are looking for. After your site has come online, you'll have actual data—in the form of server logs—to rely on. Prior to that, however, seeing into the future takes a crystal ball. You'll have to make some predictions—of which some may come true, while others may never reach fruition. In hindsight, your early hypothesis may be so far off as to prove laughable. Therefore, don't be afraid to take a stab at it. Do your research, look at peer sites, query your potential audience, and make an informed prediction.

Research Your Audience

Your research can take many forms. Sit where your audience sits. You want to learn what they're looking for. After you've spent a sufficient amount of time, you should be able to identify their needs. You can query people through email, via Web forms, through direct mail, by phone, or through participation in mail lists or bulletin boards. You might even lurk in the background on competitors' forums. Sit back and watch what's going on—you don't need to participate. Soak up all that information. Learn from it. Use it. What are your competitors doing right? What are they doing wrong? What could they be doing that they aren't?

As you do your research, you'll learn more and more about your potential audience. The dynamics of community interaction are intriguing. You'll soon be able to identify the hot heads, the shills, and the truly helpful. Some folks can't help themselves; they vent in their posts like Old Faithful lets out a plume of steam. Don't get caught up in their flames. Pay close attention to the real questions and answers. Don't hesitate when you can chime in to help. In short, people are combing the Internet looking for answers to solve their problems. Your success will come when you can solve the problems of those who would come looking for you.

Why Will They Come?

You must visualize the great motivator that will bring visitors to your front door. Think from your visitors' perspectives. Put yourself in their seats. They are out on the Internet looking for something. Something that you need (and may have on-hand) to offer. What is it?

Keep Them Content With Content

Your content is your site's greatest lure—no tricks or gimmicks, just the goods. Provide your audience with the information they seek. Do so in a clear, concise manner. Play it straight, and your audience will find *you*.

Lay out the information in a clean, concise manner. Provide as much information as you can, while maintaining a high level of quality. Web content should be as carefully written and edited as that destined for publication in a printed medium.

The Lure Of Goodies

Everyone wants a freebie, right? This isn't always the case. The person looking for free stuff is not necessarily the same person you're looking for in your audience. Make sure that you match any free offers to the demographic you seek to attract.

How Will They Find Your Site?

You don't want your site to be the best-kept secret on the Web. As you begin to plan your Web site, you must also begin thinking about the methods that you'll use to funnel traffic to the site. The following section lays out a number of crucial steps.

Get A Really Great Domain Name

There's something to be said for an excellent domain name. Although sometimes, it seems that all the great names have been snapped up! Short, sweet, memorable, and to-the-point names are often impossible. Thinking differently pays off; try combinations of words with many variations. After you have made a list of possibilities, go online and check to see what's available. Several services will query the InterNIC registry to see whether your desired domain name is available. When you find a domain name that fits, and is available, you should consider registering it immediately.

HUNT FOR DOMAIN NAMES

Network Solutions:

www.networksolutions.com

I've registered a few domain names over the years. Although I don't consider myself to be a domain-name speculator, I do enjoy collecting these great names. My biggest coup was geekbooks.com, which I registered as my personal domain name. At the time, I was amazed that no one had nabbed the "geekbooks" domain. It continues to amaze me that no one has stepped forward to offer millions for the domain name. I guess it doesn't pay to be delusional!

A few months back, I found what I thought was the perfect domain for my business. The name came on a whim, and when I checked that afternoon, it was free and clear. I hesitated to register the domain, however. Two weeks later, I decided to quit procrastinating and went to register the name. I was shocked to find out that a company in Washington State had snatched the domain name, just days before. The early Net bird catches the domain worm.

Play The Search Engine Game

The search engines are key. Unless you have invested heavily in promotion and marketing, the majority of folks will find your Web site through a search engine. And best of all, they are usually free (although that's not always the case). You need to design your site so that it is search-engine friendly. And then, you need to make sure that you register your URL with all the major search engines. *Search-engine friendly* means the following:

- *Compensates for frames*—Many search engines may have problems with indexing framed Web sites. Some strategies provide proper indexing, however. Chapter 7 provides some hints on how to handle framed sites.

- *Uses accurate page titles*—Don't forget to give each page an accurate, descriptive title.

- *Has proper META tags*—The META tags should accurately represent the page. The description and keyword tags should be fine-tuned for each page.

Webify Your Real-World Promotions

Your Web site's URL should be an integral part of your promotional plan. Although all the people in the world aren't going to stop what they're doing as soon as they hear that you have a new Web site, you do want to make sure that they can find the site when they do come looking.

You should include your URL wherever your organization would include its phone number. This includes the following locations:

- *Phone directory advertising*—Print it big and bold, just below your phone number.

- *Print advertising*—Make use of newspaper, magazine, newsletter, tradeshow, and directory advertisements.

- *Broadcast advertising*—Radio and television advertising can be brutally expensive. Make the most of your marketing dollars by including your URL at the end of each radio or TV spot.

- *Letterheads and business cards*—Don't let a single piece of stationery be reprinted without your URL.

- *Promotional items*—Suitable trinkets run the gamut from pens and calendars through baseball caps and T-shirts.

- *Press releases*—Include your URL in any corporate background information, in addition to placement on the letterhead. Publications are likely to run your URL along with any mention.

As the Web becomes more and more ubiquitous, printed phone directories will shrink. Companies will reduce the size of their printed phone book advertisements, while including their URLs in the ads themselves. Customers will go to the Web to research the firms that interest them.

Similarly, the Web will reduce the size and scope of printed brochures and catalogs. Companies will reap the rewards of lower printing and mailing costs, while being able to offer their full-blown message and product lineup online.

Consider Online Advertising

Getting the word out online can be expensive and inefficient. Banner advertising can burn cash at a frightening rate. You need to take a highly targeted approach. See Chapter 10 for a discussion of various forms of Internet advertising.

click here **PLEASE!**

Foster Links

Really great links to your site can be as important as search engine listings. Keep in mind that your site will probably never be on top of every single search engine, but links on popular sites can bring an immense level of traffic. A simple mention in a news story on a large site can bring a virtual flood of visitors.

So how do you get these great links? Follow through on all the items mentioned previously. In particular, do the following:

- Create a great site filled with wonderful content.

- Register the site with all the major search engines.

- Send out relevant press releases.

Can You Make It Happen?

Be honest with yourself. Do you have what it takes to produce the Web site you picture in your mind's eye? Does the site require more talent, resources, and expertise than you possess? The beauty of the Web is that it has absolutely no barrier to entry. Anyone who wants to post a Web site can—at absolutely no cost. Posting takes nothing more than a text editor and a little knowledge of HTML to build the most basic page.

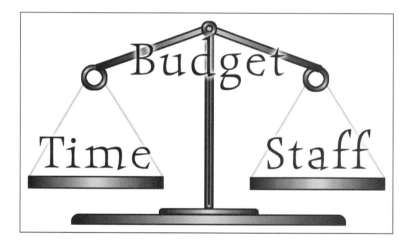

Balancing Needs

Web sites do not get built out of thin air. You need to balance your staffing and budgetary requirements to meet the implementation schedule. Let's take a look at some of the key issues.

Determine Staffing Requirements

Does your organization have the staff it needs to create this Web site? If no trained staff is on hand, you need to make a decision on how to proceed:

- *Train existing staff*—Look for staff members with enthusiasm for the project, as well as a bit of technical background and design sense. Keep in mind that not everyone has a technical background, nor is everyone a designer.

- *Out-source development*—Can you send the whole package out to an independent developer? When you're starting from ground zero, a highly skilled vendor can turn the project around faster than you can in-house.

- *Use a consultant*—Have a Web-design firm create your templates and get you started. Then, use in-house staff to build on the template and maintain the whole enchilada.

If you take a staffer away from an existing project, how will that affect others? This question needs to be answered before you progress further.

Lay Out A Budget

Do you have money in the budget to do the job right? If no money is available in the budget, you need to decide from where you can borrow it. Consider the costs for the following factors:

- *Personnel*—Can you handle the project with the folks in-house? Will you need to hire part-timers or free-lancers?

- *Hardware and software*—Are your machines up to snuff?

- *Web-site hosting*—How much will hosting the site cost?

- *Training*—Consider costs for seminars, books, and online courses.

- *Consultants*—If needed, send in the hired guns!

Estimate Time Frames

Do you have enough time to get the job done? If time frames are tight, consider increasing the staff, which means (of course) upping the budget. Don't think solely about the time required to get the site ready for launch. Think about what is required to keep the site up-to-date on an ongoing basis. When you make your first-time estimates, make sure that you pad the hours. Jobs generally take a bit longer than you initially think they will.

Be sure to budget adequate time for the following factors:

- Design

- Content creation

- Production

- Maintenance

Assessing Computing Resources

Take a look around your office. Do you have the computing resources you need to launch your Web site? Do you have both the software and hardware muscle to get the job done? If so, after you build your site, will you have the server and Internet connection reliability to maintain a constant Web presence?

Software

One of the most intriguing aspects of Web design is that it literally takes nothing to get started. With a PC or Mac and access to the Internet, you have everything you need to build a simple Web site. A basic text editor such as Notepad or WordPad (PC) or SimpleText (Mac) and a little HTML knowledge are all that you need to create a basic page.

If you have graphics software capable of creating GIF or JPEG files, you're ahead of the game. If you don't, a number of no-cost options are available, as follows:

- Download artwork from graphics-archive Web sites.

- Create artwork online.

- Download shareware graphics software (to try before you buy).

As your needs and budget increase, you can look into specialized Web site design software. Coding HTML from scratch with a basic text editor may be free, but it's not the fastest route to a highly polished Web site. It's likely that you will look into specialized WYSIWYG (what you see is what you get) Web site design software. If your needs are basic, you might start with entry-level products such as Adobe PageMill or Microsoft FrontPage. As your design needs increase, you can look into the high-end solutions, such as Adobe GoLive or Macromedia Dreamweaver.

You'll probably want to invest in some Web graphics software, in addition to Web site design software.

Hardware

Although Web design doesn't take an insanely powerful computer, you'll be happiest with a machine with a little muscle and a fast Internet connection. In general, you should use a machine with plenty of free RAM and a nice big monitor. Working with 16MB of RAM and a 13-inch monitor will get you nothing but frustrated. The more, the merrier!

If you are working on a beefy machine with a huge monitor and a cable modem, do not forget those less fortunate than you. Although you might be designing on a computer equipped with a 19-inch monitor, your visitors may be surfing on a computer with a basic low-end 13-inch monitor and a clunky 28.8 modem. I talk about designing for the lowest common denominator in Chapter 6.

Hosting

The majority of Web sites are hosted on servers outside the originating organization, for good reason. Properly administering a Web server takes a significant amount of resources. If your organization has those resources in-house, that's cool. If not, you should seriously consider having your Web site hosted at an Internet Service Provider (ISP) that specializes in Web hosting.

The ISP should provide a number of hosting plans, one of which should fit your needs. Generally, the plans include a set amount of hard-drive space, as well as a defined number of file transfers and mailboxes. By using an outside host, you can more easily budget your expenses. Hosting plans are typically offered on a month-by-month basis, although some ISPs might offer a discount on yearly contracts.

Check out this handful of national Web hosts:

- Concentric Network—**www.concentrichost.net**

- Hiway Technologies—**www.hiway.com**

- Interland Web Hosting—**www.interland.net**

- ValueWeb—**www.valueweb.net**

- 9NetAvenue—**www.9netave.net**

You also might want to look at local ISPs to see what kinds of hosting plans they offer. No matter which ISP you choose, you should always seek redundancy in its Internet connections and full backup protection on its servers. If a Net connection goes out or the ISP loses power, you want to know that your Web site will remain online 24/7, 365 days a year.

Moving On

Like the architect, the professional Web designer must fully understand the needs of the client before a successful plan can be drawn. To this end, this first chapter provided the basics of purpose, intent, and needs assessment. In Chapter 2, you'll begin to learn about the intricacies of designing Web pages and the limitations of type on the Web.

TYPE ON
THE WEB 2

Don't confuse the Web with the printed page.

The Web provides an instantaneous communication system that is wide open yet fraught with the problems brought on by inconsistent viewing systems. This chapter lays out the basics of type on the Web, helping you to avoid the pitfalls, steering you to typographic success. It starts with some of the basics of Hypertext Markup Language (HTML) text and eases into the high-end solutions.

The initial design of HTML didn't include any provision for the display of specific typefaces. Although HTML allowed authors to specify bold, italic, and regular fonts, these attributes were applied generally. In the early days, authors couldn't tell the browser to use, say, Helvetica Bold Italic. Along the way, the developers added the means to specify fonts with the <**FONT FACE**> tag. This tag allows you to *suggest* a specific font to the browser. But there's a big problem with that.

It All Depends On The Browser

HTML pages are rendered at the whim of the browser. You can code yourself blue in the face, including all your favorite fonts in your pages, but if the browsing computer doesn't have these typefaces loaded, all your carefully coded text will be displayed in the browser's default font.

Let's take a step back from the problems associated with fonts for a moment, and turn our attention to the powerful formatting that HTML provides.

Basic Text Formatting

HTML uses both *character styles* and *paragraph formats*. The difference between the two is that a character style affects selected characters only. A paragraph format, on the other hand, affects an entire paragraph. Character styles are used within a paragraph to bring emphasis to a particular word or phrase, as when the title of a book, such as *Looking Good On The Web*, is set in italics.

The three basic types of paragraph formats are as follows:

- *Heading* formats

- *Body text* formats

- *List* formats

A properly structured Web page should make efficient use of the various formats. HTML formatting commands allow Web-page text to follow a logical structure. Now, let's examine each of these formats.

> # Heading
>
> **Body** text comes in many forms. This is the most basic of all--paragraph text.
> The following three entries are set in a **list** format.
>
> - Cows
> - Sheep
> - Goats

Heading Formats

HTML provides six logical heading formats (from largest to smallest):
<H1>, **<H2>**, **<H3>**, **<H4>**, **<H5>**, and **<H6>**. (Note that **<H5>** and **<H6>**
are smaller than the body text format.) Because heading commands are
paragraph formats, they affect everything in a text block, from one paragraph return until the next. Therefore, you cannot assign a heading style
to selected words within a paragraph. When you're assigning a heading
format, you must place the starting and ending heading codes before and
after the text block, respectively. The coding looks something like this:

```
<H1>Here's The Heading</H1>
```

> # Heading 1
> ## Heading 2
> ### Heading 3
> Heading 4
>
> Heading 5
>
> Heading 6

Paragraph Formats

HTML's default **<P>** paragraph format uses nonindented text, set in a
plain roman font. In practice, you'll use the paragraph format for most of
the text on your Web pages, although you might apply different character styles and type sizes. In addition to the default paragraph style, two
special types of body text are available.

The preformatted text format **<PRE>** is handy for displaying large blocks
of text in a monospaced typeface. It's often used to create crude tabular
text without using the table commands. Every character in a monospaced
font takes up the same width, as opposed to a proportionally spaced font,
in which the *I* is much thinner than the *W*, and so on. This characteristic
enables you to create quick and dirty tables—as if on an old typewriter—
simply by using the spacebar to line up columns. The address text format

<ADDRESS> is used to denote "mailto" address lines—for the purpose of soliciting visitor feedback via an email link—which usually appear in an italic typeface.

```
This is the standard paragraph format. It's the most common form of body
text. This is the standard paragraph format. It's the most common form of
body text. This is the standard paragraph format. It's the most common
form of body text.

This is the Preformatted text format. It is set in a
monospaced font and perfect for quick and dirty tables.

1. Red Shale          1.50 per rock    $175 per palette
2. Blue Stone         1.75 per rock    $195 per palette
3. Yellow Sandstone   2.25 per rock    $235 per palette

This is the Address format. It's commonly set in an italic typeface.
```

List Formats

Several list formats are available for use in various situations. These formats are detailed in the following table:

The List formats.

Format	HTML	Result
Bullet	<UL>	Indented and bulleted.
Directory	<DIR>	Indented and bulleted.
Menu	<MENU>	Indented and bulleted.
Numbered	<OL>	Indented and numbered.
Term	<DT>	Used together with the definition format. Set on the left margin.
Definition	<DD>	Indented text, used together with the term format.

Although the first three formats appear to be identical, the difference between them has to do with the theoretical structure of the document. In practice, however, you'll use the bulleted list format more than any of the other bulleted formats.

```
• Bullet List - One
• Bullet List - Two
• Bullet List - Three

• Directory List - One
• Directory List - Two
• Directory List - Three

• Menu List - One
• Menu List - Two
• Menu List - Three

1. Numbered List - One
2. Numbered List - Two
3. Numbered List - Three

Term List - One
      Definition List - One
Term List - Two
      Definition List - Two
Term List - Three
      Definition List - Three
```

CHARACTER STYLES: PHYSICAL OR LOGICAL?

Character styles can be either *physical* or *logical*. Physical styles tag specific words with specific font attributes, such as bold or italic. Logical styles tell the browser what the intent of the text is rather than define a particular type style. Physical styles appear in the browser as the Web-page designer intends for them to appear. If you assign a bold style to a chunk of text, you can rest assured that it will be bold when it appears in your visitors' browsers. In contrast, text assigned a logical style can vary in appearance from browser to browser, depending on how the browser's preferences are set.

If you're confused by all this information, you're not alone. It's enough to know that you can play it safe by assigning physical styles rather than logical styles. If you want some text to appear in bold, make sure that you use the bold style. Don't leave your typographical decisions to the whims of the browser.

Physical Character Styles

You can use five physical character styles—plain, bold <B>, italic <I>, underline <U>, and teletype <TT>. All these styles are likely familiar, with the exception of teletype. The teletype style is similar to the Preformatted body text format. It uses a monospaced (as opposed to proportionally spaced) font, such as Courier. The following figure shows the physical character styles.

Logical Character Styles

Because there are seven logical character styles, there's a fair amount of overkill with regard to the limited set of typefaces. Some of the character styles share the same kind of typeface, as you can see in the following table.

The logical character styles.

Style	HTML	Result
Strong	<STRONG>	Usually a bold typeface
Emphasis	<EM>	Usually an italic typeface
Citation	<CITE>	Usually an italic typeface
Sample	<SAMP>	Usually a typewriter typeface
Keyboard	<KBD>	Usually a typewriter typeface
Code	<CODE>	Usually a typewriter typeface
Variable	<VAR>	Usually an italic typeface

The following figure displays the seven logical character styles.

Additional Text Controls

A highly designed Web page calls for enhanced control over text attributes other than those governed by paragraph formats and character styles. These additional text controls include the following:

- *Text alignment*
- *Text indent*
- *Text size*
- *Text color*

Text Alignment

Web-page text can be left-aligned, right-aligned by using **<P ALIGN= RIGHT>**, or centered by using **<CENTER>**. (HTML doesn't support full justification.) Text is set left-aligned by default. HTML also provides control over text alignment as it relates to inline graphics as well as text wrapping (where text appears to flow around a graphic), as is shown in Chapter 5.

Left Aligned

                    Centered

                                        Right Aligned

Text Indent

The **<BLOCKQUOTE>** command provides basic text indents from both the left and right margins. Using **<BLOCKQUOTE>** more than once indents text further and can be used to set off passages of text, as shown in the following figure.

This text is set full to the margins. It extends to the width of the browser window, wrapping when it reaches the right margin.

This text is indented once with the <BLOCKQUOTE> command. It is indented equally from both the left and right margins.

This text is indented twice with the <BLOCKQUOTE> command. It is indented equally from both the left and right margins.

Text Size

You don't need to assign a heading style if you just want to change the type size of a block of text (and especially if you don't want the text to be bold). Basic HTML allows only seven type sizes; the **<FONT SIZE="X">** command doesn't offer much flexibility. Text size choices are relative to the base font. As such, the higher the base font is set, the fewer the choices you get when you try to increase the size of a chunk of text.

This is Paragraph Text, set -2.

This is Paragraph Text, set -1.

This is Paragraph Text, set at the default.

This is Paragraph Text, set +1.

This is Paragraph Text, set +2.

This is Paragraph Text, set +3.

This is Paragraph Text, set +4.

Assigning a larger type size to a block of text within a paragraph alters the line spacing (or leading) for the lines on which the text appears. This change results in a noticeably uneven, even visually disturbing, look.

This is an example of the uneven line spacing that is introduced by enlarging the text size within a paragraph. The first two lines are evenly set. Look at what happens next ... Here is the larger text. You will notice that the line spacing has been opened up for that single line. This uneven effect is something that you will probably want to avoid. Note that smaller text within a line does not affect overall line spacing.

Text Color

You can assign color to text by means of RGB hexadecimal equivalents. The specifications are made on a page-by-page basis, within the <**BODY**> tag. The four different classifications of text, with regard to color, are body text, unvisited link, active link, and visited link. The following are the basics of each of the choices, which are detailed in the following table:

The text-color choices available in HTML.

Style	HTML	Result
Text color	<TEXT>	You'll usually use one color for all the nonlinked text on a page. Although you can set individual passages of text in a different color than the body text, these different colors can confuse the readers. Many folks assume that text of a different color is linked. They'll click and click on the colored text, to no avail.
Unvisited link color	<LINK>	This is the color of the link before it has been clicked.
Visited link color	<VLINK>	This is the color of the link after it has been clicked.
Active link color	<ALINK>	This is the color of the link when it is clicked.

The <**BODY**> tag is placed immediately after the </**HEAD**> tag. Here's an example of a <**BODY**> tag with all of the color attributes specified:

```
<BODY TEXT="#000099" BGCOLOR="#ffffff" LINK="#009999"
ALINK="#00ff00" VLINK="#00ffff">
```

Although you can go wild choosing a set of text colors to match your Web site's overall color scheme, there's a widespread acceptance that many Web surfers are confused by anything other than the default link colors. Chapter 4 dives into the topic of color on the Web (and explains those cryptic color codes).

Low-End Type Solutions

As I mentioned at the beginning of the chapter, HTML allows the designer to designate specific typefaces. Once again, the vicious truth is that although you can designate the typefaces, you have no guarantee that your visitors will have your chosen typefaces installed on their computers. This sad fact of Web life severely limits your typographical choices for HTML text.

In the early days of the automobile, Henry Ford exclaimed that his customers could purchase their Model Ts "in any color, as long as it's black." In the early days of desktop publishing, designers often joked that their clients could have "any typeface, as long as it's either Times Roman or Helvetica" (two of the core Apple LaserWriter PostScript fonts). The choices are not that much better on the Web. The only fonts you can (almost) rely on to be installed are those that come with Microsoft Windows or the Macintosh System—as well as the fonts that may be loaded with the browser. Having only these fonts available severely limits your typographical choices. The table on p. 25 displays the most common Macintosh and Windows fonts.

The table on p. 25 displays the most common Macintosh and Windows fonts.

WANT SOME NICE, BASIC WEB FONTS?

If you're looking to expand your type selection, and you're looking for fairly ubiquitous (and free) typefaces, check out Microsoft's "TrueType core fonts for the Web" at **http://www.microsoft.com/truetype/fontpack/win.htm**.

This page features a host of free fonts for both Macintosh and Windows, including Andale Mono, Webdings, the Trebuchet MS family, the Georgia family, the Verdana family, Comic Sans and Comic Sans Bold, Impact, the Arial family, the Times New Roman family, and the Courier family.

This Headline Is Set In Verdana

The body text is set in Verdana, as well. This font was designed with online readability as a prime consideration. Verdana is a big open sans serif face.

This Headline Is Set In Trebuchet MS

The body text is also set in Trebuchet MS. Like Verdana, Trebuchet MS was designed with online readability as a top consideration. Trebuchet is noticeably tighter than Verdana. It offers a higher character count per line.

This Headline Is Set In Arial

The body text is set in Arial, too. Arial is a nice clean sans serif font. It falls between Verdana and Trebuchet MS in terms of widths and character count. Some folks perceive Arial as being similar to Helvetica, but a closer look shows that it is far more squared.

This Headline Is Set in Helvetica

The body text is set in Helvetica, as well. Helvetica is a classic sans serif font--perhaps the most widely used sans serif of all time. Helvetica is nearly ubiquitous on the Macintosh, much less so on Windows.

Common Macintosh and Windows fonts.

Platform	Serif	Sans-serif
Macintosh	Times, Times New Roman	Arial, Helvetica, Verdana
Windows	Times New Roman	Arial, Verdana

Gracious Typeface Specification

Typefaces are typically specified within the HTML code using the <FONT FACE> tag, although they can also be specified within a Cascading Style Sheet (more on that, momentarily). To specify Verdana as the typeface, you set the tag to read <FONT FACE="**Verdana**">. It's a good idea to provide for computers with differing font collections. Be courteous to your visitors and avoid specifying a single face. Instead, provide an alternative (or two) by coding the tag in a manner similar to <FONT FACE="**Verdana, Arial, Helvetica**">.

Type As Graphics

Rest assured that any typeface you use in a GIF or JPEG graphic will appear as it should, regardless of the fonts installed at the browser. The ultimate flexibility of bitmapped graphics allows you to portray type as art rather than simply as a collection of characters—for example, a drop shadow floats this headline off the page. Whereas this chapter focuses on text as text, subsequent chapters go into greater depth on the subject of designing and using typographic images.

Fonts Can Make Or Break A Page

Typeface selection can set the tone for your Web pages as much as any other graphical element, be it a subtle background or beautiful illustration. Choose a headline and display font that breaks from the norm. Do some research on the Web, find the right font, and pony up the bucks to add a new typeface to your collection.

Type talks to us in ways we may not perceive. Put yourself in the role of the movie producer. When a producer casts a movie, he or she has a number of different actors come in to read the script. Although the script remains the same, each actor brings a different inflection and personality to the part. When a designer creates a site, he or she might audition a number of fonts until choosing the typeface worthy of the starring role.

Type can be subtle; it can be harsh. It can carry a mood and impart a flavor. The proper typographical choices are a matter of both taste and practicality. Body typefaces should be specified from the fonts contained in Table 2.1. Stepping too far away from these common choices is an assurance that your visitors' experience will not closely match the designer's expectations.

What Makes A Great Web Font?

When you're choosing body text, falling on the side of readability never hurts. A font that works great in print might not make the transition to the Web. High-resolution printers are kind to well-crafted typefaces. The fuzzy reality of the computer monitor doesn't come close. It has only so many pixels to construct each character. You can expect only so much. Perhaps someday soon, we will use monitors with resolutions that rival those of a laser printer. Until then, it's best to forgo the most delicate type in favor of those typefaces that were designed with screen display as their primary purpose.

Mixing serifs and sans serifs is perfectly acceptable—when done in an appropriate manner. For real-world examples of how the professionals do this, examine some magazines, scan your local newspaper, or study the pages of this book.

Try A Headline In A Sans Serif Font

And your body text in a serif face. This can impart a look not unlike that of a daily newspaper. The contrast between headline and body text adds variety to the layout without a heavy-handed effect. This example uses Arial as the headline font and Times New Roman as the body text.

High-End Type Solutions

The computer software industry loves to trumpet solutions years before their time. In hindsight, the press releases issued years ago by companies such as Adobe and Microsoft read as inaccurate a prediction of the future as those made by a boardwalk fortune teller. It has been three years, as this is written, that Adobe and Microsoft proposed to merge PostScript and TrueType into the OpenType format. As of this writing, this promise has failed to have an impact on the world of Web typography.

Let's look at a scheme that *has* affected the way Web sites are formatted.

Typographical Control Via Cascading Style Sheets

Cascading Style Sheets (CSS) allow you to achieve a higher level of control over type specifications. With a style sheet, you can define the body

LOCATING TYPE ON THE WEB

The Web presents a plethora of places to preview and purchase typefaces. Here's a short list:

- **www.eyewire.com**
- **www.fontshop.com**
- **www.itcfonts.com**
- **www.philsfonts.com**
- **www.typeindex.com**

and heading specs just once on a page (or for an entire site)—rather than each place the typeface appears. This way, you can easily edit and update pages. The word *cascading* refers to the scheme's hierarchy—one style is often based on another. Changes in the first style trickle down to the second (and third, and so on)—governed by the specifications within each.

The first version, CSS-1, was implemented by the World Wide Web Consortium (W3C) in late 1996 and gained widespread support in Netscape Navigator 4 and Microsoft Internet Explorer 4. The second version, CSS-2, was implemented in the spring of 1998. Older browsers do not support the CSS standard; keep this point in mind if you are building a site that might be viewed by a good number of visitors using other than the latest and greatest browser.

Let's look at some of the high-level typographical controls afforded by CSS:

- *Fonts*—Specify entire font families (Arial, Helvetica, Times, and so on), as well as styles (bold, italic, roman, bold italic, and so on), weights (lighter or bolder), and size (in your choice of points, pixels, absolute, and relative terms).

- *Colors*—Define text as well as the text background color by RGB (hexadecimal) specifications or keyword.

- *Word and letter spacing*—Affect the interword and intercharacter spacing.

- *Margins*—Independently set the left, right, and top margins.

- *Borders*—Place an optional border around a chunk of text (in lieu of using a single cell table).

Chapter 11 revisits the topic of Cascading Style Sheets, with a focus on formatting and positioning.

Adobe Acrobat

The Adobe Acrobat Portable Document Format (PDF) provides a platform-independent means to exchange documents among Macintosh, Windows, and Unix systems. If you need to put documents on your Web site that will be printed on your visitors' printers, your needs are best served by Adobe Acrobat. With Acrobat PDF, the documents will print with fidelity. The layout will be intact, complete with fonts, images, and razor-sharp vector graphics. Printing HTML Web pages, on the other hand, relies on whatever fonts are on the visitors' computers, with graphics limited to low-resolution bitmaps.

LOOKING FOR THE W3C CSS-1 AND CSS-2 SPECS?

Check out the following links:

www.w3.org/TR/REC-CSS1

www.w3.org/TR/REC-CSS2

WHAT ABOUT EMBEDDED FONTS?

The concept of *embedded fonts* allows a font (or number of fonts) to download to the browser along with a Web page. In theory, this capability sounds pretty cool—a page will look exactly as its designer intended. Although Microsoft introduced the capability to embed TrueType fonts in Web pages with Internet Explorer 4, the concept didn't take off.

The Acrobat Reader can be installed as a Web browser plug-in. This way, your visitors can view Acrobat PDF files without launching the Acrobat Reader separately. So, what kinds of documents are Acrobat PDF fodder? A good time to use PDF is when you're creating the following:

- Complex reports
- Business forms
- Scientific white papers
- Text with mathematical annotations
- Highly designed marketing material
- Product-specification sheets
- Newsletter archives
- Documentation

Adobe Acrobat PDF Files

Acrobat files can begin life in just about any program, from QuarkXPress to Microsoft Excel. Adobe PageMaker 6.5 can create Acrobat PDF files right out of the box. If you're not using PageMaker (or another program capable of creating PDF files directly), you need the full version of Adobe Acrobat to create PDFs. The full version of Acrobat might set you back a couple of hundred bucks, whereas the Acrobat Reader is distributed for free. Buying the full version is a small investment that can pay itself back many times over.

The full version of Adobe Acrobat comes with two tools, PDF Writer and Acrobat Distiller, which are used to create Acrobat PDF files.

PDF Writer

PDF Writer is installed in the same manner as a printer driver. When you're ready to create your PDF file, you target and print to PDF Writer as a virtual printer from within the application. This way, you can create PDF files in one step. PDF Writer is intended for the creation of basic PDF files on the fly.

Acrobat Distiller

Acrobat Distiller is a standalone application. Unlike PDF Writer, Acrobat Distiller requires a two-step process. First, the original application file is printed to a PostScript file. Then, the PostScript print file must be run through Acrobat Distiller to create the PDF file. Distiller is intended to handle all types of pages, from the simplest to the most complex. It can operate on a file-by-file basis or in batch mode.

ADOBE ACROBAT WEB RESOURCES

Check out this short list of online Acrobat resources, from FAQs and Web zines through Acrobat plug-in developers:

- *Acrobat FAQs—* **www.blueworld.com/ acrobat.faq.fcgi**

- *Acrobat Talk Mailing List—* **www.blueworld.com/ blueworld/lists/ Acrobat.html**

- *Adobe Systems—* **www.adobe.com/ prodindex/acrobat/ main.html**

- *Ambia—* **www.ambia.com/**

- *Emerge PDFZone—* **www.pdfzone.com/**

- *EnFocus—* **www.enfocus.com/**

- *Lantana—* **lantanarips.com/**

- *PurePDF—* **www.purepdf.com/**

- *xman software—* **www.xman.com/**

Moving On

When it comes to typography, the Web leaves much to chance. As a Web designer, you must minimize the odds. By choosing your fonts carefully from those most commonly found and by specifying alternative fonts, you stand to achieve a higher degree of graphic fidelity. The options afforded by Cascading Style Sheets and the widespread adoption of the CSS standards promise greater reliability.

Although this chapter touched on the subject of color on the Web, Chapter 4 goes into depth on the topic, with 16 pages of full color.

BUILDING
FORMS

3

Although forms are far from glamorous, they are a pivotal means of Web interactivity.

Do you hear that whooshing sound? The World Wide Web is a giant vacuum cleaner, sucking up information at an astounding rate. This massive influx of data is largely made possible through the use of HTML forms. HTML forms allow information, entered at the browser, to instantaneously reach the server. This basic interactivity has been a core success of the Web revolution. Unfortunately, the topic of HTML forms is often one of the most daunting concepts for the neophyte Web designer to grasp. This chapter will ease into the topic without overburdening you with technical issues.

You might want to use HTML forms for a great number of reasons. The following are some common examples:

- Product or service order forms

- Information request forms

- Contest entry forms

- Guestbook entry forms

- Navigational elements

Learning How Forms Work

HTML forms generally work in one of three ways. They either interact with a Common Gateway Interface (CGI) program at the server, they work with a database application at the server, or they contain JavaScript that enables the forms to operate without interacting with the server (although the data might be submitted to a CGI). The program (whether it's a CGI script at the server or JavaScript built into the form) interprets the information entered into the forms and acts on the data it receives.

Form Elements

All forms must begin with the <**FORM**> tag and end with the </**FORM**> tag. Nine additional HTML form elements are available. Forms can use any or all of these elements. Each form element has a name and a value, and you have complete control over how these variables are labeled. It's essential that you assign consistent names and values to each. Don't confuse the title (that you see on the Web page) with the actual name of the form element. Although visitors to your site see the title, the CGI sees the actual name.

HTML form elements put interface-building tools into the hands of nonprogrammers. Let's take a look at each of the form elements before diving further into the topic of CGI and JavaScript.

Checkboxes

Click here! Checkboxes are often set as groups, which allow any, all, or none of the group to be selected. The following snippet of code shows the input type set to **checkbox** and the name set to **wood**. The common name defines each element as being part of the **wood checkbox** group. **CHECKED="1"** denotes **maple** as the default checkbox.

```
<P><INPUT TYPE="checkbox" NAME="wood" VALUE="cherry"> Cherry</P>
<P><INPUT TYPE="checkbox" NAME="wood" VALUE="maple"
CHECKED="1"> Maple</P>
<P><INPUT TYPE="checkbox" NAME="wood" VALUE="oak"> Oak</P>
```

Checkbox:

☐ Cherry

☑ Maple

☐ Oak

Radio Buttons

Click here, too! Radio buttons are similar to checkboxes, with one important difference (besides their shape). Although radio buttons are also set as groups, only one radio button in a group can be selected at a time. Once again, the common name defines each element as being part of the **siding** radio button group. **CHECKED="1"** denotes pine as the default radio button.

```
<P><INPUT TYPE="radio" NAME="siding" VALUE="cedar">
Cedar</P>
<P><INPUT TYPE="radio" NAME="siding" VALUE="cypress">
Cypress</P>
<P><INPUT TYPE="radio" NAME="siding" VALUE="pine"
CHECKED="1"> Pine</P>
```

Radio Button:

○ Cedar

○ Cypress

● Pine

Text Fields

Text fields are used to enter single lines of text. **SIZE** denotes the length of the text field. Be sure to leave enough room for longer entries.

```
<P><INPUT TYPE="text" NAME="textfieldnamegoeshere"
SIZE="30"></P>
```

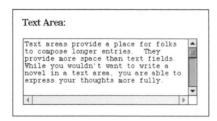

Text Areas

Need more than just one line of text? Use a text area if your visitors will be entering a larger chunk of text. By using **ROWS**, you can specify the depth of the text area. By using **COLS**, you can specify the width of the text area. **WRAP**="**PHYSICAL**" is optional; it allows the text to wrap in the box as it is entered.

```
<P><TEXTAREA NAME="textareanamegoeshere" ROWS="10" COLS="40"
WRAP="PHYSICAL"></TEXTAREA></P>
```

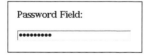

Password Fields

The password field might look a lot like a text field, but it's used for just one purpose—to enter a password. When your visitors type their passwords into a password field, the browser displays bullets in lieu of letters or numbers.

```
<P><INPUT TYPE="password" NAME="andthepasswordis" SIZE="30"></P>
```

Drop-Down Menus

HTML forms provide two ways to select information from lists: drop-down menus and scrolling lists. Drop-down menus allow your visitors to make just one selection; they do not allow multiple-choice entries. (Drop-down menus may also be referred to as pop-up menus.) When a visitor clicks on the list, it drops down, displaying all the selections on the menu.

```
<P><SELECT NAME="Fasteners">
<OPTION VALUE="drywall nails" SELECTED>Drywall Nails
<OPTION VALUE="finish nails">Finish Nails
<OPTION VALUE="roofing nails">Roofing Nails
</SELECT></P>
```

Scrolling Lists

You can configure scrolling lists to allow your visitors to make one or a number of selections. **MULTIPLE** denotes the ability to make multiple selections. **SIZE** denotes the number of lines displayed. The list does not scroll if the size equals the total number of lines.

```
<P><SELECT MULTIPLE SIZE="3" NAME="tool department">
<OPTION VALUE="hand tools">Hand Tools
<OPTION VALUE="tool boxes">Tool Boxes
<OPTION VALUE="power tools">Power Tools
<OPTION VALUE="accessories">Accessories
<OPTION VALUE="blades and bits">Blades and Bits
</SELECT></P>
```

The order of entry in the code determines the order of display in the Web browser. This order also holds true for both drop-down menus and scrolling lists.

Hidden Fields

Hidden fields are invisible in the Web browser (although they are visible when viewing the HTML source code). The purpose of a hidden field is to send information (other than that entered into the fields, checkboxes, and radio buttons) along with the submitted form. This information can include the submitting page or other data.

Reset Buttons

Reset buttons are meant for convenience. They allow the visitors to clear a form automatically. You can alter the text on the Reset button by changing **VALUE="Reset"** to **VALUE="whatever you would like"**.

```
<INPUT TYPE="reset" NAME="resetme" VALUE="Reset">
```

Submit Buttons

When clicked, the Submit button sends the information in a form to the server. It is required on every form. You also can alter the text on the Submit button by changing **VALUE="Submit"** to **VALUE="whatever you would like"**.

```
<INPUT TYPE="submit" NAME="submitme" VALUE="Submit">
```

CGI: The Smarts Are At The Server

A form merely provides the means of gathering information. You need to have a CGI script or other program running on your Web server before you can do anything with the submitted data. The CGI must know what to do with this information, and it must be in sync with the form so that it understands what to do with the various names and values. Note that CGI scripts are server-specific. A script written on one platform might not run on another. Unix Perl, for example, might not work properly on a Windows NT Server.

If HTML forms seem mysterious to the neophyte Web designer, CGIs can seem positively otherworldly. However, they don't have to be; if you need to implement a CGI script on your Web site, your first stop should be with your Webmaster or service provider to find out what kind of support is available. There may be existing scripts that you can adapt for your use. If not, you might find what you need from the scores of CGI scripts available on the Web.

CGI Resources

The Web is one of the best places to find scripts. For more information about CGI scripts and for downloadable scripts you can use "off the rack," check out this trio of popular CGI resource sites:

- *Matt's Script Archive*—**http://www.worldwidemart.com/scripts/** This Web site features some popular CGI scripts, including Guestbook, WWWboard, Counter, Formmail, Random Image Displayer, Random Link Generator, Simple Search, and Free for All Links.

- *BigNoseBird.com CGI Script Archive*—**http://bignosebird.com/** This Web site provides a nice selection of interesting scripts, including NoMoDoMo E-Mail Subscription System, BNB Virtual Greeting Card Server, BNB All-in-One Form Processing, BIRDCAST Site Reader Recommendation, BNBBOOK Guest Book, BNB Domain Name Lookup, and BNB Banner Rotator.

- *ScriptSearch*—**http://www.scriptsearch.com/** This immmense Website library consists of thousands of CGI scripts. You can find scores of scripts for handling ad banners, bulletin boards, calendars, guest books, mail utilities, redirection, security, tracking, and much more.

JavaScript: Magic In The Browser

Adding JavaScript to forms can help to clean up the data before it is submitted. Forms can be scripted to contain error checking and validation. Although JavaScript wasn't supported by the early Web browsers, support today is practically universal. The topic of JavaScript is touched on in Chapters 7 and 9.

JavaScript Resources

Again, the Web is the best place to look when you need JavaScripts. Check out this trio of popular JavaScript resource sites:

- *JavaScript Source*—**javascript.internet.com/** Hundreds of handy cut-and-paste JavaScripts are brought to you at this site, courtesy of internet.com.

- *Javascripts.com*—**www.javascripts.com/** Now owned by EarthWeb, this site hosts thousands of JavaScripts.

- *CNET Builder.com SuperScripter*—**www.builder.com/Programming/Kahn/** This very cool site builds custom JavaScripts for you, based on your input.

Server-Based Applications

Although the majority of Web server interactivity has historically used CGI scripts, heavy-duty server-based applications have exploded onto the scene. If your needs go past the basics, and you are aiming for serious database interactivity, you will have to pay the piper and buy into a program, such as those mentioned below in "Popular Server-Based Applications."

Popular Server-Based Applications

Once again, go to the Web to find applications if you are a true power user. The following four server-based applications are the most popular:

- *Allaire ColdFusion*—**www.alliare.com** A popular choice for server-based application development, ColdFusion uses its own language, Cold Fusion Markup Language (CFML), in lieu of more intricate programming languages.

- *Apple WebObjects*—**www.apple.com/webobjects** Apple bought this application (along with Steve Jobs) when it purchased NeXT.

WebObjects was the original Web-application server platform and has been used to build thousands of high-end Web sites.

- *Elemental Drumbeat*—**www.drumbeat.com** Drum roll, please! This product has garnered wide acclaim for its ability to quickly create database-driven Web sites with Active Server Pages (ASP).

- *Microsoft FrontPage*—**www.microsoft.com/frontpage** This highly popular Web authoring program enables you to provide discussion forums, handle form data, and provide text searches through FrontPage Server Extensions. (Your ISP, however, must support the FrontPage Server Extensions.)

Designing Forms

Although you might think of forms as nasty little pieces of necessity, great form design truly is an art. You will find that the time you take to create a form that has been fully conceptualized is time well spent. The difference between a poorly executed and a carefully executed form can sway your users' experience. A form provides yet another choice between torturing your audience and treating them well. The Golden Rule, "Do onto others as you would have them do onto you," applies here.

Easy To Navigate

After a visitor fills out the first field in a form, he or she can use the Tab key to navigate through the fields. The form should be logically organized to meet the expectations of the user. The order in which you need your data might not match this organization. Get over it! Set up your form so that it's as easy as possible to navigate. You can fiddle with the data after it gets to the server.

Precisely Aligned

You have no excuse for creating a sloppy form. Text fields and areas should align horizontally, whenever practical. Use consistent spacing between checkboxes and radio buttons. For more control, use HTML tables to lay out your forms with precision. The following two figures and accompanying code demonstrate the simple difference between a rough form and an organized form. Which would you rather fill out?

```
<P>Name:<INPUT NAME="Name" TYPE="text" SIZE="35"><BR>
Address 1:<INPUT NAME="address1" TYPE="text" SIZE="35"><BR>
Address 2:<INPUT NAME="address2" TYPE="text" SIZE="35"><BR>
City:<INPUT NAME="city" TYPE="text" SIZE="35"><BR>
State:<INPUT NAME="state" TYPE="text" SIZE="35"><BR>
```

```
Zip Code:<INPUT NAME="zip" TYPE="text" SIZE="35"><BR>
Telephone:<INPUT NAME="phone" TYPE="text" SIZE="35"><BR>
Fax:<INPUT NAME="fax" TYPE="text" SIZE="35"><BR>
Email Address:<INPUT NAME="email" TYPE="text" SIZE="35"></P>
```

Name: [   ]
Address 1: [   ]
Address 2: [   ]
City: [   ]
State: [   ]
Zip Code: [   ]
Telephone: [   ]
Fax: [   ]
Email Address: [   ]

```
<TABLE BORDER="0" CELLSPACING="2" CELLPADDING="0">
  <TR><TD ALIGN="RIGHT">Name:</TD>
    <TD><INPUT NAME="Name" TYPE="text" SIZE="35">
</TD></TR>
  <TR><TD ALIGN="RIGHT">Address 1:</TD>
    <TD><INPUT NAME="address1" TYPE="text" SIZE="35">
</TD></TR>
  <TR><TD ALIGN="RIGHT">Address 2:</TD>
    <TD><INPUT NAME="address2" TYPE="text" SIZE="35">
</TD></TR>
  <TR><TD ALIGN="RIGHT">City:</TD>
    <TD><INPUT NAME="city" TYPE="text" SIZE="35">
</TD></TR>
  <TR><TD ALIGN="RIGHT">State:</TD>
    <TD><INPUT NAME="state" TYPE="text" SIZE="35">
</TD></TR>
  <TR><TD ALIGN="RIGHT">Zip Code:</TD>
    <TD><INPUT NAME="zip" TYPE="text" SIZE="35">
</TD></TR>
  <TR><TD ALIGN="RIGHT">Telephone:</TD>
    <TD><INPUT NAME="phone" TYPE="text" SIZE="35">
</TD></TR>
  <TR><TD ALIGN="RIGHT">Fax:</TD>
    <TD><INPUT NAME="fax" TYPE="text" SIZE="35">
</TD></TR>
  <TR><TD ALIGN="RIGHT">Email Address:</TD>
  <TD><INPUT NAME="email" TYPE="text" SIZE="35">
</TD></TR>
</TABLE>
```

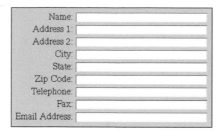

Easy To Read

Build your forms with readability in mind. Use generous type sizes. A form is no place for "the fine print." Link to the boilerplate information and FAQs on another Web page, rather than reducing the size of the type to fit.

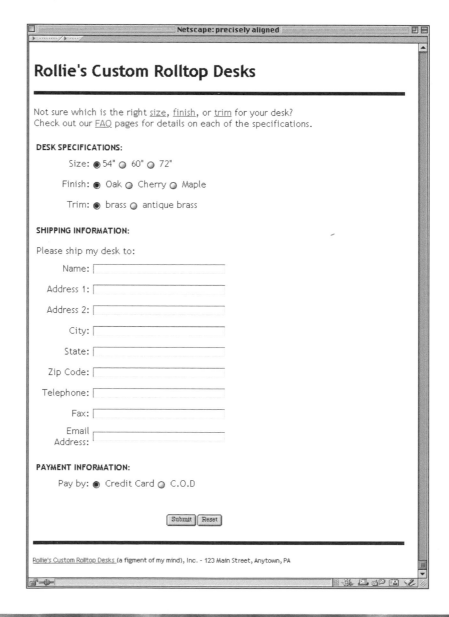

Self-Explanatory

Avoid ambiguity. Include helpful hints and links to pertinent help information on your forms. You want to make your forms so easy to use that your grandparents could fill them out. To achieve this goal, you can beta-test the forms with a select group of people.

Just The Right Size

Don't overwhelm your visitors; avoid huge scrolling forms. You want your forms to be easily digestible. If you have an extremely long form, consider breaking it into a series of separate pages.

Include Error-Checking

Use JavaScript to verify fields before they are submitted. Doing so helps to avoid missing, erroneous, or fraudulent data. Plenty of canned JavaScripts are available to check for the validity of specific data.

Not Boring!

The more interesting a form, the better chance it has to be filled out. Although you cannot expect Web forms to be as exciting as a theme park thrill ride, they don't have to be boring gray pages, either literally or figuratively. For example, you don't have to use those standard dull gray buttons; you can always design your own graphic buttons instead.

A Little Courtesy Goes A Long Way

Be polite to your guests! Build your forms with sufficient room in the text fields and with the **WRAPPING** option in text areas. Remember your common courtesies—please and thank you.

Consistent Style

A form should not stand out from the rest of the Web site. Maintain a consistent style with regard to backgrounds, text color, and graphics.

Careful Execution

Check your forms carefully before going live. Run tests from a variety of browsers and from both Windows and Macintosh platforms. Then, make the changes needed to allow a pleasing view on all the Web browsers.

Moving On

Forms are all about moving information! In this chapter, you learned how Web forms work and how you can make them work for you. In Chapter 10, you'll learn about the many types of Internet advertising and how you can best market the Web site that had its beginnings in this chapter.

The next chapter goes into depth on color, with 16 pages interspersed with color examples.

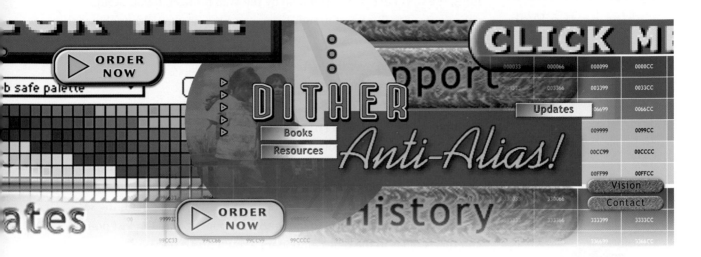

COLOR ON
THE WEB

4

This chapter sheds light on the mysterious world of color on the Web.

To the newcomer, the world of Web color can be an unpredictable place. The color you specify on your computer might not look the same way on your visitor's computer. Does this theme seem familiar? Like the world of fonts, the world of color is governed by the Web browser. If you design your pages with this point in mind, you can have greater, although never total, control over the results.

Let's start by going over the Web color basics.

Web Color Basics

Remember your color wheel from grammar school? Web color works in a similar manner. All Web colors are created through a combination of red, green, and blue (RGB) and are specified via hexadecimal RGB equivalents. These hexadecimal codes can look cryptic, but they're nothing to fret over. The first pair of characters refers to the red component, the second pair of characters refers to the green component, and the last pair of characters refers to the blue component. (You'll find a two-page chart of colors and codes later in this chapter.)

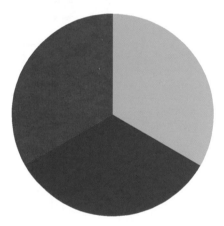

HEXADECIMAL RGB COMPONENTS

The following hexadecimal codes represent the pure on-screen components of RGB:

- #ff0000 = Red
- #00ff00 = Green
- #0000ff = Blue

You can include color information in a Web page in a number of ways. HTML enables you to change type color, background color, and table cell colors. Of course, you also can use lots of color in your GIF and JPEG graphics. But, direct coding of color in the HTML source is the fastest way to a colorful page. With all the color contained in the code, the browser doesn't have to download and render anything else. As you can see in the following figure, Dan's Internet Fence Supply shows two different color table treatments, with the columns and rows delineated with color, respectively. Table color is specified in a cell-by-cell basis, as in <TD BGCOLOR="#99cc99">.

Note: *Because of inherent differences between how color is handled onscreen and on the printed page, you may notice subtle (and occasionally, not-so-subtle) shifts when comparing printed material (such as the color in this book) to similar colors on your computer's monitor. It's much like comparing apples and oranges—neither will ever look exactly like the other.*

The page background color, body text color, link color, and visited link color are specified within the <**BODY**> tag. In the case of Dan's Internet Fence Supply, only the background color and link text color were specified as follows:

```
<BODY BGCOLOR="#66cccc" LINK="#660066">
```

All the other choices were left as the default colors. The following body tag defines the text, background, normal link, and visited link color:

```
<BODY TEXT="#000099" BGCOLOR="#ffffcc" LINK="#cc3300"
VLINK="#cc9900">
```

Using colored table cells, you can create interesting pages without spending days designing graphics in a separate program. In the example on page 46, the cells in the top row of the table are assigned a dark brown background color, while the first column (with the exception of the uppermost cell) are assigned a dark red background color. The remainder of the table cells are left uncolored, so that the page background color shows through. Chapters 6 and 7 cover the subject of Web-page layout and design.

CAN'T DEAL WITH THE CODES?

You don't have to hack out that hexadecimal code. All the modern Web-page editors provide a visual means to specify color.

SO WHAT ARE THE DEFAULTS?

You can override the default colors by changing the browser preference settings. Most often, they are left at the original settings:

- *Background*—Most often gray or white

- *Body Text*—Black

- *Normal Link*—Blue

- *Visited Link*—Purple

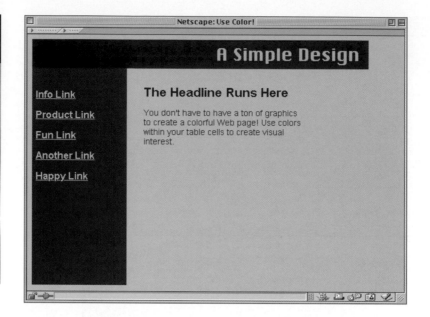

Why Color Differs From Computer To Computer

The two basic reasons behind the unreliability of Web color are monitor gamma and video display color depth. Understanding the differences between these two factors will help you to choose the optimal colors for the widest range of browsers.

Gamma Correction

Gamma correction is a system correction made to affect the brightness of the monitor. The standard Macintosh gamma is 1.8, whereas the standard Windows gamma is 2.5, which makes the Macintosh display brighter than the Windows display. Because of this difference, graphics designed on a Macintosh tend to appear muddier and darker when you view them on a Windows computer. And consequently, graphics designed on a Windows computer tend to appear lighter and washed out when you view them on a Macintosh. The image shown on the left is a little washed out, while the image on the right is a bit too dark (see next page). Gamma also affects the relationship between the red, green, and blue component colors; this change in the relationship can alter the overall hue, in addition to the brightness.

Although you (as a Web designer) may not be able to preview your creations on both Windows and Macintosh platforms, you can take some steps to compensate for this difference. One of the most common strategies is to create your graphics with Photoshop (or your tool of choice) set to a gamma of 2.2—halfway between the Macintosh and Windows standard settings.

Color Depth

Modern computers are equipped with video systems that can display either 24-bit (millions of colors), 16-bit (thousands of colors), or 256 colors. The number of colors displayed is referred to as *color depth*. Color depth is determined by the computer's video card, video-display driver, and monitor. The more colors your computer can display, the better your images will appear. Color-depth settings can be specified via your computer's Control Panel. On a Macintosh, you need to use the Monitor Control Panel. On a Windows machine, you need to use the Display Control Panel.

The differences between the video display color depth of the browser can lead to annoying dithering and color shifts. These color shifts can affect GIF and JPEG graphics alike. Your gorgeous 24-bit color scans degrade and dither when viewed on a computer with a lowly 256-color display. Thankfully, 16-bit displays fare far better than do their lowly 256-color brethren.

GAMMA LINKS

You can refer to these pertinent links regarding gamma correction:

- Builder.com: Web Graphics 101, Color matching and gamma correction— **http://builder.com/ Graphics/Graphics101/ ss04.html**

- CGSD: Gamma Correction Home Page— **www.cgsd.com/ papers/gamma.html**

Here's a photograph as displayed in 24-bit color:

The image begins to degrade in 16-bit color:

Dithering is evident in 256 colors:

A "zoom-in" on the image demonstrates exactly what's happening. The 256-color Web browser throws a spray of dithered colors—completely ruining an otherwise nice-looking photo. Just look at those spots; they're worse than a case of the chicken pox!

The 256-color image is noticeably dithered:

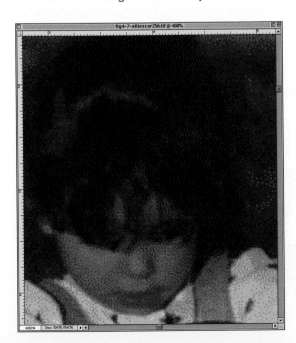

The 24-bit image is relatively smooth:

The dithering dilemma extends beyond just photographs; it affects all graphics. If you use a color that is not within the standard color palette, rest assured that it will dither.

Dithering And Non-Browser Safe Colors

Here's another look at a potential dithering problem, this time showing a GIF image created with non-browser safe colors. The first image shows the GIF as viewed on a 24-bit display. The colors are true and smooth.

Now take a look at the same image as viewed on a 256-color display. The dithering and color shift is evident. Dithering is highly noticeable in the flat color sections of the image. Check out those hideous dither patterns in the zoomed view!

The Netscape Palette

To deal with the color discrepancies between disparate platforms, Netscape designed its original Navigator Web browser (and all subsequent versions) to use a common palette of 216 colors. These colors are often referred to as being "Web safe." The colors are safe in that they do not dither when viewed on different platforms (Macintosh, Windows, and Unix) or at different color depths (with a minimum of 256 colors). Microsoft wisely chose the same exact color palette for Internet Explorer. The following spread displays all 216 colors, along with their hexadecimal values. Although accurately conveying the screen colors in print is impossible (due to the differences between additive and subtractive color), this illustration should give you a rough idea of the inherent limitations in the palette.

The Netscape palette, part 1:

000000	000033	000066	000099	0000CC	0000FF
003300	003333	003366	003399	0033CC	0033FF
006600	006633	006666	006699	0066CC	0066FF
009900	009933	009966	009999	0099CC	0099FF
00CC00	00CC33	00CC66	00CC99	00CCCC	00CCFF
00FF00	00FF33	00FF66	00FF99	00FFCC	00FFFF
330000	330033	330066	330099	3300CC	3300FF
333300	333333	333366	333399	3333CC	3333FF
336600	336633	336666	336699	3366CC	3366FF
339900	339933	339966	339999	3399CC	3399FF
33CC00	33CC33	33CC66	33CC99	33CCCC	33CCFF
33FF00	33FF33	33FF66	33FF99	33FFCC	33FFFF
660000	660033	660066	660099	6600CC	6600FF
663300	663333	663366	663399	6633CC	6633FF
666600	666633	666666	666699	6666CC	6666FF
669900	669933	669966	669999	6699CC	6699FF
66CC00	66CC33	66CC66	66CC99	66CCCC	66CCFF
66FF00	66FF33	66FF66	66FF99	66FFCC	66FFFF

The Netscape palette, part 2:

990000	990033	990066	990099	9900CC	9900FF
993300	993333	993366	993399	9933CC	9933FF
996600	996633	996666	996699	9966CC	9966FF
999900	999933	999966	999999	9999CC	9999FF
99CC00	99CC33	99CC66	99CC99	99CCCC	99CCFF
99FF00	99FF33	99FF66	99FF99	99FFCC	99FFFF
CC0000	CC0033	CC0066	CC0099	CC00CC	CC00FF
CC3300	CC3333	CC3366	CC3399	CC33CC	CC33FF
CC6600	CC6633	CC6666	CC6699	CC66CC	CC66FF
CC9900	CC9933	CC9966	CC9999	CC99CC	CC99FF
CCCC00	CCCC33	CCCC66	CCCC99	CCCCCC	CCCCFF
CCFF00	CCFF33	CCFF66	CCFF99	CCFFCC	CCFFFF
FF0000	FF0033	FF0066	FF0099	FF00CC	FF00FF
FF3300	FF3333	FF3366	FF3399	FF33CC	FF33FF
FF6600	FF6633	FF6666	FF6699	FF66CC	FF66FF
FF9900	FF9933	FF9966	FF9999	FF99CC	FF99FF
FFCC00	FFCC33	FFCC66	FFCC99	FFCCCC	FFCCFF
FFFF00	FFFF33	FFFF66	FFFF99	FFFFCC	FFFFFF

Getting More Color

The 216-color Web palette is the bane of many a serious Web designer. There's just not enough color! Programmers and designers have striven to surpass the limitations of the palette since they were first brought to light. Thankfully, a workaround is available for the dithering problem. You can build custom patterns using Web-safe colors; the colors in these patterns blend together to create new colors, which the eye may perceive as pure (when viewed at normal size). This method is intended for use with GIF images rather than JPEG images. It's ideal for creating custom Web page backgrounds in which you want a specific color (rather than a wacky texture).

Using BoxTop Software's ColorSafe (**www.boxtopsoft.com**) is one of the most popular methods for creating custom color patterns. ColorSafe creates patterns in 2×2, 3×3, 4×4, 5×5, 6×6, and 8×8 grids; it works with any graphics program capable of using Photoshop plug-ins.

Creating the Web-safe color in ColorSafe:

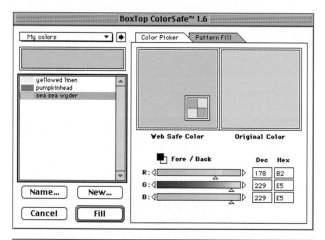

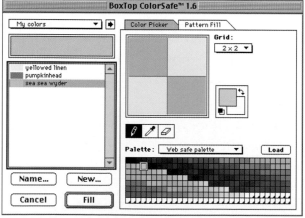

A zoomed view of the Web-safe color pattern, showing the individual pixels. This fine pattern dither will be imperceptible to the eye when viewed at 100 percent.

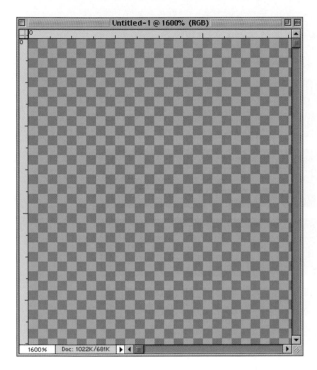

The downside to this method is that the patterns should be used only within individual GIF graphics or as the GIF page background. Patterns should not be used as table cell backgrounds because support for this attribute is not universal. Although the newer Web browsers support table cell background graphics, the older browsers do not.

Striving For Readability

Your visitors should never have to struggle to read your Web pages. The colors you select, along with the typographical specifications, are of chief concern. The text and background colors should provide sufficient contrast. In general, we are accustomed to reading black text on a white background. Although this combination works on paper, the computer display cries for a slightly different treatment. A bright-white background isn't the easiest on the eye. A subdued off-white or subtle tint can be much easier to tolerate. Although the Web-safe palette doesn't offer many choices, you can build your own colors with tools such as BoxTop Software's ColorSafe.

> **Dark blue (#000033) on pale yellow (#ffffcc)
> takes off the edge**

> **Dark blue on light green (#99cc99)
> is soft and easy**

> **Dark blue on tan (#cccc99)
> lends a distinguished look**

> **Pale yellow on purple (#330033)
> is a little rough on the eyes**

> **What about the same pale yellow
> on dark blue?**

> **And why not pale yellow on dark red (#330000)?**

Choosing Color Schemes

So, where do you find a great color scheme? The answer depends on whom you have to keep happy! If you are designing Web pages for corporate clients, chances are that the marketing department already *has* a color scheme in mind. Straying from those corporate colors can give the heebie-jeebies to weak-kneed middle managers. So, if you have to design in corporate land, design as those in corporate land do: Conform or risk being demoted to the mailroom! In all seriousness, if corporate standards are in place, you would be wise to heed them. But, if a client comes asking for more, pulling a tasty color scheme out of your hat can't hurt. (I can write this scenario because, in my case, it's "been there, done that!")

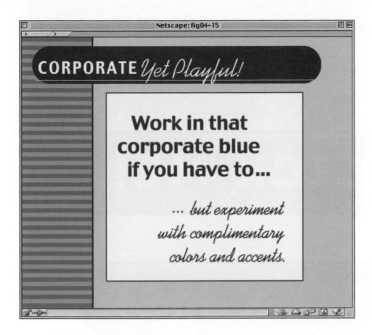

Less Color, More Speed

In the beginning of this chapter, I suggested that you can have plenty of color and still have a fast-loading Web page. It's important to use HTML color in backgrounds and table cells to your best advantage. When you build GIF graphics, use the fewest number of colors possible to achieve your desired effect. Cutting down on the number of colors shaves graphics file sizes, which results in speedier downloads. Rectangular elements often result in smaller files than curved elements because the curves require greater numbers of colors to achieve a smooth result. In this example, the rounded-corner button uses a greater number of colors in order to *anti-alias* the rounded edges to the background color.

Try to use flat color whenever possible. Three-dimensional effects—such as beveled or embossed buttons and navigational elements—tend to create larger graphics files. The number of colors can increase substantially. (The examples shown here use an excessive number of colors.)

Moving On

When everything is said and done, Web color is a crapshoot. In this chapter, you learned about the basics of Web color, as well as some of the issues related to cross-platform color and image fidelity. The next chapter tackles the topic of Web graphics, covering the different varieties of graphics and graphics file formats.

GETTING STARTED WITH GRAPHICS

Give your readers some eye candy by incorporating graphics into your Web pages.

Graphics are the building blocks of Web design. When used correctly, graphics transform a page from a dry text-only experience into a captivating combination of text and graphics that can boost both comprehension and usability. This chapter will cut through the confusing topic of Web graphics, as it defines the different types of graphics and explains how you can use each most effectively. You'll learn how to choose the best format for your images, along with GIF and JPEG image compression tips.

Graphics And Their Uses In Design

Let's take a moment to examine the general classes of Web graphics. Identifying each of the elements is the first step in understanding their specific roles and functions.

The most basic types of Web graphics include the following:

- *Identity graphics*—Tell who you are. Identity graphics include corporate and product logos.

- *Structural graphics*—Form the overall shape of the page.

- *Navigational graphics*—Provide a way to get from here to there.

- *Contextual graphics*—Tie directly to page content.

- *Ornamental graphics*—Embellish the page design without adding considerable content.

These classifications of elements are most often used in concert with one another. A navigation bar, for example, usually integrates site identity into the navigation structure because it provides navigational links to other pages within the site. As another example, you can use ornamental icons as hyperlink buttons to deliver site navigation without a hard-edged button look.

Identity Graphics

Your organization's logo, if it has one, should be carried on each and every page on your Web site, in precisely the same location and size. You should reap a number of benefits from following this practice:

- *Consistency*—The logo can help you provide visual continuity from page to page. As your visitors move through your site, they will feel a sense of coherence and order.

- *Back door coverage*—Having the logo on every page helps visitors familiarize themselves if they enter your Web site through a page other than the front page. Visitors frequently enter this way when they are referred to a specific part of your Web site via a search engine or a link on another site.

- *Branding*—The more frequently that visitors see your logo, the more familiar they will become.

OUT IN LEFT FIELD

Logos are most frequently located in the upper-left corner of the page, emulating a printed letterhead. It's a common practice to link this logo to the front page of the Web site.

Structural And Navigational Graphics

Structural and navigational graphics usually work hand in hand. The structure exists to carry the links (often in the form of buttons) as well as to provide a setting for the page content. Chapter 4 introduced the concept of using colored table cells to create page structure. Pure table-cell layouts consist of flat, hard-edged color. By using graphic images, you can build more dimension into your designs.

You can take your pages to the next level by using structural graphics within the cells to soften the hard edges and add the illusion of curved surfaces. These graphics include the text, which is hyperlinked via an image map.

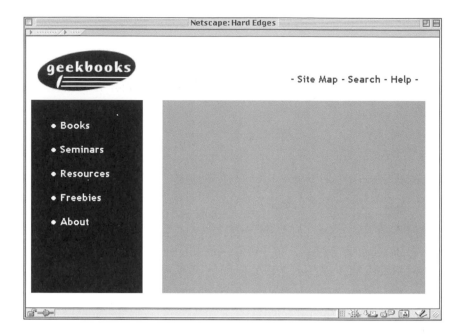

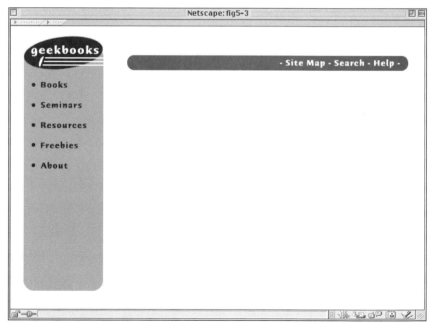

Navigation Bars

Navigation bars can have either a horizontal or vertical orientation.
Many pages use both horizontal and vertical navigational elements, as
demonstrated by these basic illustrations. As graphic elements grow in
complexity, they are sliced into pieces to fit into the table layout. Chapters 6 and 7 go into greater depth about the topics of page structure and
navigational systems.

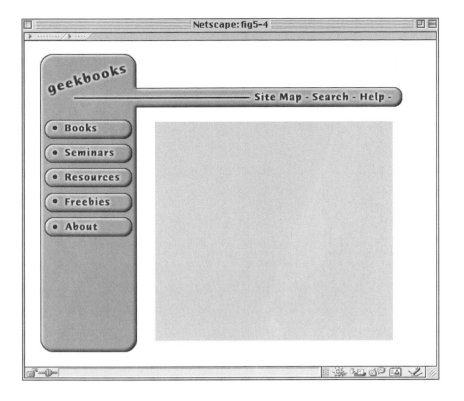

Buttons

Our pushbutton world has carried over from real life onto the Internet. Where once a simple highlighted text link was enough to take us from one page to another, now we expect an experience that echoes our existence at the keyboard. Web buttons can take many forms—from simple, flat objects to lush, three-dimensional designs that appear to be pressed down when the cursor passes over them.

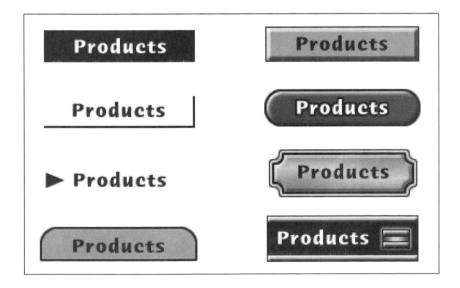

Metaphors are everywhere. Some Web buttons look like the buttons that control household appliances, audio-visual gear, and automobiles. Others look like file folder tabs or mimic computer program interface components, which are themselves merely an emulation of tools we use in real life.

Dividers

HTML provides for basic horizontal divider bars with the **<HR>** command. You can use these four different specifications:

- *Size*—You specify the number of pixels (for example, **<HR SIZE="3">**).

- *Width*—You specify the number either in pixels or as a percentage of page width (for example, **<HR WIDTH="400">** or **<HR WIDTH="80%">**).

- *Shading*—Horizontal rules are shaded by default. (For example, you use **<HR NOSHADE>**.)

- *Alignment*—You can set alignment to left, right, or center (for example, **<HR ALIGN=RIGHT>**).

The built-in HTML rules, if used correctly, are subtle. Of course, you can also use graphic horizontal rules. By doing so, you can fully control the color, shape, size, and style of the rule.

Contextual Graphics

Contextual graphics add real content. They relate closely to the text, helping to tell a story or depict a concept. Great graphics—whether illustrations or photographs—explain by example. The successful combination of both text and contextual graphics increases reader comprehension levels. An expressive illustration or an impeccable photograph can convey more information to the visitors in one glance than a Web page chock full of text. The old adage "A picture is worth a thousand words" is true—however, only if it's the *right* picture. Take the time to find or create the right picture, and you will be rewarded. If you use what you have at hand just to fill space, netizens will scoff and your Web site will wither.

Illustrations

By using custom illustrations, you can convey information or mood that you may not be able to convey by text alone. Illustrations—unless they are highly realistic—must be interpreted by the readers. The most appropriate and effective artwork is created specifically for the need at hand. For this reason, it's a prudent business decision to find the right artists and have them render something according to your needs. If you have a budget to spend on real illustrations, get your hands on a bunch of artists' sourcebooks or scour the artists' Web sites. Custom illustration may cost more than stock illustration, but the added expense can be money well spent.

ILLUSTRATION SOURCES

Check out these illustration Web sites (note that these sites represent working artists, and the images presented here are for sale):

- **www.artville.com**
- **www.artwanted.com**
- **www.zaks.com/ illustrators/**

Photographs

Photographs are among the most compelling Web graphics. More than any other type of imagery, photographs quickly tell their story. By conveying a sense of reality, photographs place the viewers right into the picture and leave little to interpretation (unless, of course, the photos are abstract).

You should carefully choose and prepare photographs for Web use. Images should be cropped for maximum impact and sized for minimal download time. Contrast and brightness should be adjusted for a broad range of displays.

Clip Art

Clip art is the staple of designers faced with a deadline crunch. If the time or budget fails to allow for a custom illustration or photograph, clip art often gets the nod. Although using clip art can be fast and easy, it often fails to portray the design with the proper intent. Choosing the right artwork is not always an easy task. Often, the artwork you have in mind is impossible to find. If you have a wide range of high-quality clip art at your disposal, you have a big advantage.

CLIP ART SOURCES

Check out these clip art Web sites:

- **www.arttoday.com**
- **www.clipartdownload. com**
- **www.rtcomputer.com**

Charts

Charts enable you to convey data quickly in a compact, visual manner. When turned into a chart, information that is laborious to pore through in columnar form can be comprehended in seconds. Web charts can come from a wide variety of programs ranging from specialized charting applications to spreadsheets. The more sophisticated applications should be able to export charts in the proper file format (most often GIF). However, a program does not need export capabilities. Anything that you can display on your computer screen can be turned into a graphics file simply by using a quick screen-capture method or application.

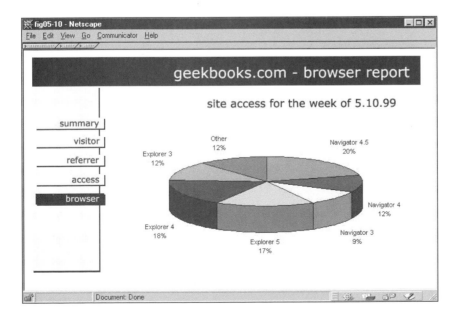

CONSIDER A SCREEN CAPTURE UTILITY

If you need to perform many screen captures, it's a good idea to invest in a screen-capture utility. These programs can automate the process of capturing images and converting file formats.

Screen Captures

Screen captures (frequently called *screen grabs*) are easy to perform on both Macintosh and Windows computers. You use screen captures when creating online documentation for desktop applications. To perform a screen capture, you can press Cmd+Shift+3 on the Macintosh or press PrtScn for full-screen captures in Windows 98 (pressing Alt+PrtScn in Windows 98 captures just the active window). Macintosh screen captures are stored as PICT format files, whereas Windows screen captures are stored as BMP format files. These files should be converted into GIF format before you incorporate them into a Web page.

Sizing can be a problem when you're using screen captures in Web page designs. You should set the screen resolution of the computer used for the capture to 640×480 to avoid grabbing too large an image. (Screen captures can be difficult to scale down.)

Ornamental Graphics

Generally, ornamental graphics are not essential to the information on a given page. They're meant to help convey a mood or feeling as they add visual interest to the design. A page can exist without ornamentation, as the best pages often do. Let's look at dingbats and icons—the two most common forms of ornamental graphics.

Dingbats

Dingbats are diminutive illustrations, stored as fonts. They are most often used as small ornaments within a block of text. One of the most popular applications is to use a dingbat in lieu of the standard HTML bullet. When you use a dingbat as a bullet, you have full control over color, shape, and size.

DING DING DING!

Where do you find *your* dingaling(bats)? This Web site is a great place to start:

• **dingbats.i-us.com**

You shouldn't specify a dingbat font by using the HTML **FONT** tag. Instead, render the dingbat as a graphic image with your favorite graphics program. Then, place the dingbat into the HTML text by using an **IMG SRC** tag.

Icons

Icons are small, decorative illustrations. They are similar to dingbats, although icons are often used at a larger size and may utilize a more intricate design. Icons are frequently used as navigational elements to add a stylized or whimsical touch.

Choosing The Proper Format

GIF and JPEG are the two most popular graphics file formats for Web design. It's important to know which format to use at what times. One size doesn't necessarily fit all.

When To Use GIF

The GIF format is an *indexed-color* format. An index-color format uses a color palette of up to 256 colors per image. You should use GIF for solid-color graphics, logos, line art, and cartoon-like illustrations. The GIF format produces the best compression on images with large areas of flat, contiguous color. When possible, you should avoid using the GIF format with photographs; doing so often results in a grainy, posterized, or chunky appearance.

TEXT LINKS, TOO!

Don't expect your visitors to understand every doodle on your page. If you decide to use icons as navigational elements, it's also a good idea to include text links to the same URLs to which the icons point.

IT'S A BITMAP WORLD (WIDE WEB)

GIF and JPEG are bitmap formats—that is, these graphics formats represent an image with a grid of pixels. These two formats have been the mainstay of Web designers. Recently, the Web has seen an increasing movement to use vector-based illustrations—such as those produced by Macromedia Flash. In Chapter 9, you will take a look at this topic.

When To Use JPEG

You should use the JPEG format for photographs and other artwork with many color and tones. JPEG produces the best all-around compression with the smoothest transition between colors. Try not to use the JPEG format on graphics with large areas of flat, contiguous color; using the format this way often results in a splotchy or mottled appearance. (Look closely at the gray background in the preceding image—the second image—that surrounds the type.)

Compressing Graphics

Speed is the name of the game in Web graphics. Sharp Web designers always strive to spare their audiences from excessive page loading times. You can make Web pages download and display more rapidly by shaving graphics file sizes. Fewer bytes = better performance.

GIF Optimization Tips

Effective use of the GIF format's options can really help make your pages great looking and fast loading. Keep in mind the following basic GIF-format optimization tips:

- **Use the smallest palette you can get away with.** The fewer colors in the file, the smaller your final file will be.

- **Work with large areas of contiguous color.** The more contiguous color, the tighter you can squeeze the file size.

- **Think horizontally.** Because of the nature of the GIF format, images compress best when areas of color are contiguous horizontally.

- **Dither only when necessary.** Because dithering interrupts contiguous areas of color, it can increase file sizes.

- **Stick with browser-safe colors, when possible.** Doing so helps to avoid dithering on different computers.

- **Use the interlaced GIF89a format.** Interlacing allows an image to flow into the page as it loads. Although using interlacing is no faster than using noninterlaced images, it provides a taste of something for your visitors to see while the images are loading.

- **Experiment with GIF optimization software.** If your graphics application's built-in GIF export mechanism doesn't provide all the bells and whistles, you can find a wide range of programs that do.

JPEG Compression Tips

Keep in mind the following basic JPEG-format compression tips:

- **Use the lowest quality setting you can get away with.** Often, you can achieve a high level of compression (which translates into a faster, more efficient Web-page display) without overtly affecting the integrity of the image. Experimenting pays off.

- **Don't JPEG a JPEG.** JPEG is a *lossy* format. Lossy is a method of compression that loses some data in an attempt to eliminate redundant (unnecessarily duplicated) information in the image. Lossy techniques make the file size (not the dimensions of the image) smaller, which results in faster loading. If overdone, however, it can cause noticeable degradation of the image. Each time you save an image as a JPEG, it loses some quality from the original image. If you resave the same image as a JPEG several times, you will soon see a very noticeable degradation—similar to copying a photocopy several times.

If you are experimenting to achieve the best balance between compression and display quality, always start by copying the original image, then choose your compression options, and finally save it under another name—this way, you'll avoid unnecessary degradation.

- **Consider using JPEG optimization software.** If your graphics application's built-in JPEG export mechanism does not provide a high level of control, you can find a wide range of programs that do.

- **Use the progressive JPEG format.** *Progressive JPEGs* are similar to interlaced GIFs in that they provide something for the viewers to see as the image downloads. A progressive JPEG appears blurry when it first appears in the Web browser because it displays the entire image, minus half its total pixel count; it progressively comes into focus as the image is downloaded. Although it's not really faster than "nonprogressive" JPEG files, the psychological effect of seeing a blurry-yet-entire image makes it seem so.

  The only downside to the progressive JPEG format is lack of support in older Web browsers. This has become less of a factor over time, as netziens upgrade their browsers.

A Word About Copyright

Before you use any image on your Web site, be sure that you have the right to do so and that you understand all of the limitations and permissions associated with the image. You would be wise to check the fine print that accompanies your illustrations, clip art, photographs, and other artwork to make sure that you are not violating the rights of the creator of the artwork.

Moving On

When properly handled, graphics can turn a raw manuscript into a finished document by providing identity, structure, content, and style. This chapter merely serves as an introduction to this topic. As you progress through the rest of this book, you'll continue to acquire an increasing measure of knowledge about the nature of Web graphics. The next chapter delves further into the subject of graphics as it delivers the basics of Web page layout.

PAGE LAYOUT
BASICS

In this chapter, you'll learn about the basics of Web page layout.

Without structure, a Web page is merely an amorphous jellyfish of text and images. Jiggly and wiggly may work for the sea creature, but it isn't the best way to convey information. Structure enhances comprehension. This chapter demonstrates the many forms of page layout with HTML tables as it explains page structure and intent.

Building Page Structure

In the beginning days of the Web, all pages used a rudimentary single-column structure, with text and graphics flowing to fit the width of the browser window. Web designers gained the ability to take charge of their page layouts over time, through the adoption of new versions of HTML and updated Web browsers. As the years passed, designers moved from basic single-column layouts into more complex multiple-column designs. This evolution became possible after the introduction of HTML tables. Multiple-column layouts provide the control designers craved as Web pages evolved to mimic the printed page.

Single-Column Layouts

The basic single-column layout enforces a pure linearity to the page, with everything flowing one after another. Although pages designed in this manner seem like a throwback to the early nineties, their simplicity allows for display across the widest possible range of Web browsers. You need only a header graphic and some text to create a basic page, as shown in the first example here. Note how the text reflows into the smaller browser window in the second example.

Running Text Around Graphics

HTML has long included the capability to run text around graphics. This feature emulates the *word-wrapping* capabilities first popularized by desktop publishing software in the late eighties. A number of IMG tag options determine how text reacts to an inline graphic. The options provide for rudimentary control over image placement. You can set text to top align, center align, bottom align, left align, and right align to an image. A properly defined IMG tag calls the source (SRC) image, then sets the width and height (in pixels), in addition to setting the alignment and border options. The following code shows examples of top, middle, and bottom alignment:

```
<IMG SRC="kite.gif" WIDTH="220" HEIGHT="253" ALIGN="TOP"
BORDER="0">

<IMG SRC="partyhat.gif" WIDTH="195" HEIGHT="258" ALIGN="MIDDLE"
BORDER="0">

<IMG SRC="dance.gif" WIDTH="244" HEIGHT="257" ALIGN="BOTTOM"
BORDER="0">
```

The following code shows examples of left and right alignment.

```
<IMG SRC="fishy.gif" WIDTH="246" HEIGHT="241" ALIGN="LEFT"
BORDER="0">
<IMG SRC="sundae.gif" WIDTH="271" HEIGHT="237" ALIGN="RIGHT"
BORDER="0">
```

WHY SET THE WIDTH AND HEIGHT?

While you can use an IMG tag without setting the image's width and height, it's not a recommended practice. If you fail to insert the width and height, it slows down the page display because the browser will have to wait for the image to download before flowing the text. By inserting the width and height, you tell the browser exactly how much space to leave for the image, which enables the text to flow around the image while the image downloads.

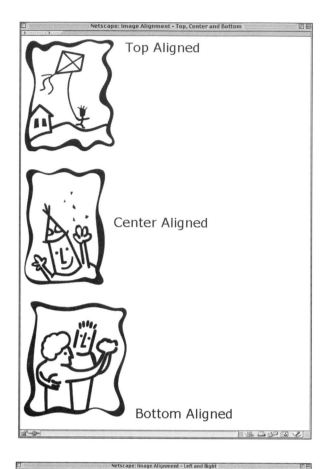

Netscape: Image Alignment - Top, Center and Bottom

Top Aligned

Center Aligned

Bottom Aligned

Netscape: Image Alignment - Left and Right

Word wrapping sets the text around the graphic. This example uses a left alignment setting to wrap the text on the right side of the graphic. Word wrapping sets the text around the graphic. This example uses a left alignment setting to wrap the text on the right side of the graphic. Word wrapping sets the text around the graphic. This example uses a left alignment setting to wrap the text on the right side of the graphic.

This example uses a right alignment setting to wrap the text on the left side of the graphic. Word wrapping sets the text around the graphic. This example uses a right alignment setting to wrap the text on the left side of the graphic. Word wrapping sets the text around the graphic. This example uses a right alignment setting to wrap the text on the left side of the graphic. Word wrapping sets the text around the graphic.

You also can govern the horizontal and vertical distance between the text and graphic by using the **HSPACE** and **VSPACE** settings in the IMG (for Image) tag, as follows:

```
<IMG SRC="standoff.gif" WIDTH="292" HEIGHT="231" HSPACE="24"
HSPACE="24" ALIGN="RIGHT" BORDER="0">
```

WHAT ABOUT JAGGED RUNAROUNDS?

Unfortunately, HTML doesn't support jagged runarounds (images are defined strictly by rectangular means). If you want to wrap text tightly around an image, you'll have to compose the text with the image as a graphic.

Constraining Single-Column Layouts

Left unconstrained, text always flows to fit the browser window width. Thankfully, you can easily control this text flow. By encasing the entire contents of the page within a single cell table, you can constrain the layout to a specific width (in pixels) or a percentage of browser width. Single-column layouts can benefit most from the percentage of browser width method. When you specify a percentage table, your page contents are held off the edges of the browser with gutters of white space. If the browser is resized, the table contents reflow to fit the new window size. Compare the text in the following example to the first two figures in this chapter. This text was constrained to 80 percent of the browser width in a single cell table.

Fixed-width tables, on the other hand, do not allow the contents to reflow if the browser window is resized. In this case, the layout appears cut off when the Web browser is set to a width narrower than the table width. Not too cool.

Multi-Column Layouts

Most current Web pages use a multicolumn layout. By using multiple columns, you can pack more information into a limited space. Two- and three-column layouts are the most popular designs. Navigational elements are usually placed into the leftmost column.

You can use table cell color to create a sense of page structure. You can also use it to accent individual columns and cells as shown in the following example:

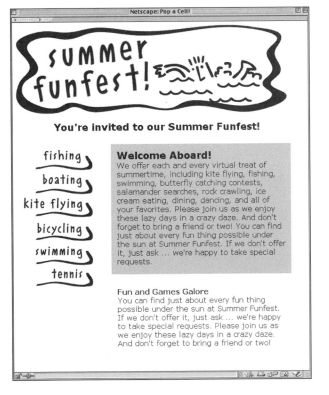

Although most multi-column page layouts might appear to be built with two- or three-column tables, this is often not the case. Page layout tables often include additional columns to establish gutters of white space between the text columns. Although the table command includes a cell padding setting, using it is not the best method to create space between text columns. The following figure shows the table setup for the previous figure as viewed in Adobe PageMill. Note the thin column between the navigational elements and the text.

Vertical dividers can serve to provide additional definition between text columns. You can create these thin vertical rules by using a slightly more complex table. Instead of using a single white space gutter column between text columns, you can use a trio of columns—two white space columns surrounding the black rule column.

SPACER GRAPHICS

Transparent *spacer graphics* are often used to help ensure that a layout holds together. These invisible images prevent tables from collapsing empty cells. Experienced designers reuse a 1x1 pixel transparent GIF throughout a page, stretching it to fit table cells, as needed.

Using Background Images

Background images set the stage for your Web-page designs by providing a canvas upon which all other elements are composed. They are rendered in the browser by repeatedly tiling an image—specified within the page's <**BODY**> tag—to fill the Web browser window. Background images are most commonly GIF files, although JPEG files can be used with current browsers. The four basic types of backgrounds are shown in the following list:

- patterns
- vertical stripes
- horizontal stripes
- big images

Patterned Backgrounds

Pattern backgrounds run the gamut from subtle repeating watermarks and embossed designs through intricate textures. You can produce seamless textures through a variety of tools—often using Adobe Photoshop or a paint editor capable of using Photoshop plug-in filters. The most popular methods include the built-in Photoshop Offset filter, Xaos Tools Terrazzo plug-in, and Kai's Seamless Welder plug-in.

The following example shows a basic embossed logo, and the next one shows a slightly funky pet-lizard seamless texture:

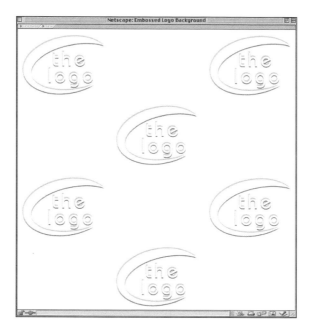

Vertically Striped Backgrounds

Variations on the vertically striped background theme are among the most popular on the Web. Scores of Web sites use a dark stripe running down the left side of the page, with a lighter (usually white) body area. The following figure of a background image (and the figure of the full-screen page that uses it) shows a basic three-stripe vertical tile used as a background image. The most basic vertically striped backgrounds use just two colors, whereas their slightly more-complex brethren add a third area, beyond 600 pixels or so, to imply a dead zone. The result can be striking, as the Web page shows.

Textured striped backgrounds can make a distinctive statement. The trick to implementing textures within vertically striped Web backgrounds is to select textures that are seamless from top to bottom. These texture tiles should be tall enough to avoid an obvious repeating pattern, yet small enough in file size to ensure a reasonable download time.

Consequently, the height of a textured-stripe background is governed by the height of the seamless texture itself. Vertical stripes often use subtle shading to create 3D effects. The shading provides the illusion of depth. Here, you can see both a three-stripe vertical tile with an interesting texture applied to the leftmost stripe, and the resulting page.

It takes a steady hand to build seamless curved stripe designs, such as in the following examples. It's imperative that the pixels match from top to bottom—otherwise, the repeating pattern will show a visible notch. You can use curved edges to create unusual and playful vertical striped backgrounds.

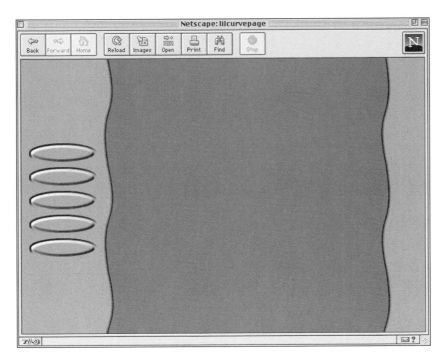

Horizontally Striped Backgrounds

Although vertically striped backgrounds are the most popular on the Web, a horizontally striped background can be a stylish and distinctive choice. Make sure that your horizontal stripe backgrounds are tall enough to avoid vertical tiling in the browser. Repeating a horizontal stripe is a design faux pas. Generally speaking, horizontal stripes work best on short pages. You need only two solid areas of color to get started with a horizontally striped tile. The horizontal stripe serves as a clean backdrop for navigational and identification graphics. Of course, you can always add a pinstripe rule or a touch of 3D to make the stripe "pop" from the page. These examples show just a portion of the horizontal striped tile.

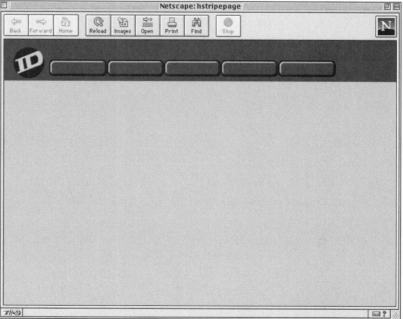

You can place objects along the dividing line between the colored stripe and body area to create interesting sawtooth-edged designs. Jaggy deckle-edge backgrounds, such as the tile shown here, offer a break from the hard-edged background patterns found on most Web pages. Patterned edges can run the gamut from saw tooth (triangles), through gear tooth (rectangles), deckle edges, and beyond.

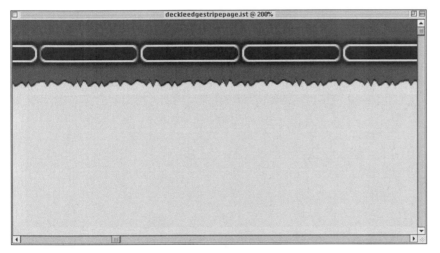

Big Image Backgrounds

Sometimes, you might want to use one large (non-tiling) background image. For a background image not to tile, it must be larger than the contents of the Web page in both dimensions. Remember, the larger the dimensions, the bigger the file, and the longer the download time. The most successful full-page backgrounds consist of just a handful of colors. Don't entertain the idea of a photographic full-page background. The file size would be impracticably large. Instead, stick with limited palette images. Watermarked and ghosted images are the most common non-tiling background images.

Some Background Info

When you're designing a tiled background image, you need to consider these three key points:

- Ensure readability.

- Avoid overly complex designs because less is more.

- Never let them see your seams.

Throughout the design stage, ensuring readability is imperative. The information contained within your Web pages is more important than the electronic paper (the background) on which it is printed. You should avoid overly complex designs because they may confuse your visitors. Wild patterns can be fun, but you should use them only where they do not obscure the text. Always strive for a clean, effective, and seamless presentation of your pages.

Accommodating Your Audience

Will your Web site play in Peoria? You can design the most eye-popping, mind-blowing, full-screen example of performance art, but if your visitors can't enjoy the same visual experience as you can, all your work will be for naught. Always put the needs of your audience first.

Design For The Lowest Common Denominator

Before you set out to design that wide-screen multimedia masterpiece, you need to consider two important questions:

- Which browsers are your visitors using?

- What display resolutions are they using?

These are two primary factors in determining your site's lowest common design denominator. Until a Web site has been up and running for a while, determining the site's lowest common Web browser denominator can be difficult. Although some folks may quote browser statistics gleaned from a magazine article or press release, those general statistics don't necessarily relate to the surfers who are visiting *your* site.

The lowest common denominator can move slowly. Many people are reluctant to upgrade their browsers. Furthermore, although browser development moved rapidly in the time when Netscape fought off the early swarm of competition, intense browser development has slowed. Although Netscape's death duel with Microsoft kept browser development on the front burner for a while, things have cooled to a simmer. The tail end of Netscape's supernova as an independent software developer (before being eaten by America Online) brought less and less of a marketing push to get folks to upgrade their browsers.

Your Web site's server logs will show what kinds of Web browsers your visitors use. Web-server-log statistical analysis tools can process the server logs and provide you with an accurate report. Determining the client computer's display resolution is a tad more difficult; Web server logs do not contain this information. To determine display resolution, you need to add a small JavaScript to selected pages. This JavaScript can create a special log file of its own.

Set A Maximum Width Of 600 Pixels (Or So)

Folks who access the Internet on a computer running a 640×480 pixel display are at a distinct disadvantage. Don't poke them in the eyes. If you design your site with a fixed-pixel width, try not to exceed 600 pixels. Be

ARE TABLES OKAY?

Rest assured that it's fine to use HTML table layouts! The number of browsers that fail to support tables is negligible. I haven't seen a version 1.0 browser rear its ugly head in the server logs in a long while.

kind to these poor souls and shave another 10 pixels if you can; 590 pixels should be a safe width for everyone.

You can set fixed-width layouts to flush-left or to float to the center of the browser window. Floating a layout to the center of the browser is a good strategy to deal with various browser widths.

Shrink (Or Expand) To Fit

You can accomplish the sacred one-size-fits-all page if you design your layout tables with percentages rather than with fixed-pixel widths. These accordion-like layouts provide for a great deal of flexibility.

Float The Cream To The Top

Want your Web site's visitors to click through? The most important item on each page should be positioned within the first 300 pixels. Make sure that your visitors see the goods; never assume that they'll scroll down the page. Why just 300 pixels? This distance (approximately) is all that's left on a 640×480 screen after you take the browser interface into consideration. Keep the display-challenged in mind.

Keep It Clean

Don't make your page layouts any more complex then they really have to be. Clean, simple pages are inherently more readable. If you think that your page has too much content, in all likelihood, that's the case. Don't stuff 20 pounds of page content into a five-pound bag.

Deliver The Familiar

A few years back, I went to Germany on a business trip. I had just begun working for a company that was exhibiting at a two-week-long tradeshow in Düsseldorf . Each afternoon when the show closed, we had a one hour bus ride from the show hall to our hotel in Cologne. Now, with the exception of a few words, I don't speak or read German. I was the proverbial stranger in a strange land. One day, I piped up as I thought we were nearing the hotel, "Hey, there's the sign for our hotel." A co-worker shot back, "What the heck do you mean?" "That sign," I said unknowingly. "Ausgang. I see that Ausgang sign every night when we get off the Autobahn." To which my co-worker graciously replied, "Ausgang? That means 'exit,' you idiot!"

The moral of the story? Don't make your visitors feel like idiots. If you attempt a complex or tricky layout and fail, you may alienate your guests. Give them a familiar layout, and they will feel at home.

Moving On

In this chapter, you learned the basics of Web-page layout through the means of HTML tables. Take charge of your page layouts, and you'll take the next step in your progression as a Web designer. The following chapter builds on the page layout basics, as it covers the topic of Web site navigational systems, image mapping, and frames.

PART II

DESIGNING FROM A STRONG FOUNDATION

NAVIGATIONAL SYSTEMS 7

Don't let visitors stumble around in the dark! Give them the means to find their way around your site.

Imagine driving into a town where none of the road signs make sense. How would that make you feel? Would you feel unsure or wary? Now, imagine landing on a Web site that makes it hard to find your way from page to page. Would you feel as if you've driven off an exit ramp into the Twilight Zone? This chapter delves into the topic of Web site navigation. It covers the basic points of navigational orientation, metaphors, interface design, and the thorny issues of designing with frames.

It's absolutely essential that *every* page of your Web site be easily navigable. A clear and consistent navigational system will foster user satisfaction and will increase the number of pages your visitors view. The easier it is for your visitors to find their way around your site, the better they'll feel about your organization.

Choosing Navigational Orientation

Before the advent of HTML table layouts, early Web sites largely used horizontal navigation systems, with the links running across the top of the page. When HTML table layout became popular, designers quickly moved to exploit the possibilities afforded by vertical navigation.

As a first step, you should assess the number of static links. How many links have to be carried on every page? The sheer number of links can dictate whether your navigational system will use either a horizontal or vertical orientation (or both).

Horizontal Navigation Systems

Placing navigational links horizontally across the top of the page makes the links immediately accessible. This approach is favored by speed-conscious site designers and is more effective with text than it is with graphic links. If your Web site has a line of text links at the top of each page, your visitors can instantly navigate through the site, without waiting for lengthy image downloads.

The downside of using a horizontal navigation bar at the top of the page is that it quickly scrolls out of view. For this reason, it's a good idea to include a second horizontal navigation bar at the bottom of the page. Graphic navigational systems allow you to tailor the interface to fit any theme. It's common to see a fancy graphic navigation bar at the top of the page, with a secondary, more austere navigation bar at the bottom of the page.

Horizontal graphic navigation bars are used most often at the top of the page, although they can also be used at the bottom of a page when contained within a static frame. The following figure provides an example of a bottom frame navigation bar. (The topic of frames is covered at the end of this chapter.)

Vertical Navigation Systems

By nature, vertical navigation bars create a layout grid in which the links are pushed off to the side in a narrow column. This arrangement serves to make the navigation links secondary to the primary content of the page. Vertical navigation systems can accommodate a greater number of links than horizontal systems, without getting too cluttered.

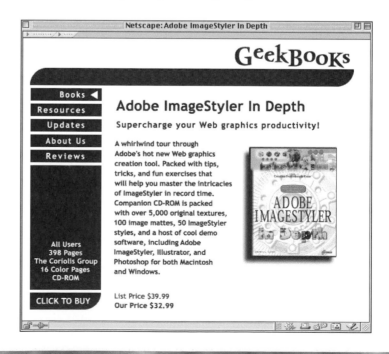

Vertical navigation bars are most frequently found at the left side of the page, although an increasing number of sites feature navigational elements on the right side of the page. The following example uses an open design with a nice amount of white space.

Vertical navigational links can quickly scroll out of view on long pages. Here, too, it's a good idea to include a second set of horizontal text navigation links at the bottom of those long pages.

Pop-Up Navigational Systems

JavaScript makes it easy for you to create compact pop-up navigational systems. These little menus save space and look slick, although they can present problems for folks surfing with old browsers that do not support JavaScript. At the risk of sounding repetitive, if you use JavaScript navigational menus, you should also include some rudimentary text link navigation hyperlinks at the bottom of the page to accommodate browser-impaired surfers.

Many JavaScript menu navigation scripts are floating around the Web. You can find a host of JavaScript resources in the appendix of this book. If you don't feel comfortable adapting scripts, you don't have to feel left out. Builder.com has a feature (in the SuperScripter section of its Web site)

called the "Menu maker" that automatically builds the scripts according to your specifications. You simply enter the menu items and URLs, select where you want the links to lead (either the same window or a new window), click a button, and then copy and paste the custom code into your Web page.

Building Image Maps

Using HTML, you can link individual images or you can assign multiple links to one (often larger) image. Images that provide more than one link use *image maps* to carry the links. Let's take a look at the difference between the two.

If an image is only linked to just one URL, you don't need to use an image map. The code for an individually linked image looks like this:

```
<A HREF="books.html"><IMG SRC="Books.gif" BORDER="0"
WIDTH="128" HEIGHT="28" ALIGN="BOTTOM"></A>
```

Books

The code for a simple image map looks like this:

```
<MAP NAME="map1">
  <AREA SHAPE="rect" COORDS="0,0,128,28" HREF="books.html">
  <AREA SHAPE="rect" COORDS="0,33,128,61" HREF="resources.html">
  <AREA SHAPE="rect" COORDS="0,65,128,93" HREF="updates.html">
  <AREA SHAPE="rect" COORDS="0,98,128,126" HREF="aboutus.html">
  <AREA SHAPE="rect" COORDS="0,131,128,159" HREF="reviews.html">

</MAP><IMG SRC="navmap.gif" USEMAP="#map1" BORDER="0" WIDTH="128"
HEIGHT="159" ALIGN="BOTTOM" ISMAP>
```

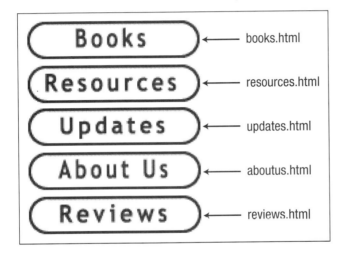

As the code demonstrates, an image map defines linked areas via pixel coordinates. Although image mapping can get fairly complex, tools built into the major Web page and Web graphic creation applications make image map creation a snap. With most programs, creating an image map is no more difficult than drawing a rectangle and assigning an URL.

Image maps can provide navigational links on photographic compositions or other artwork. Although the imagemap's hotspots are described in hard-edged vector terms, the image can blend into the background of the page. The following example uses an alpha channel matte to achieve a soft-edged appearance. Only the individual terms are linked.

SERVER SIDE, CLIENT SIDE, OR FRIES ON THE SIDE?

The two kinds of image maps are *server side* and *client side*. Early pages used the server-side method—synching up with a Common Gateway Interface (CGI) on the Web server to serve up the link. The server-side method has pretty much fallen by the wayside, as designers now primarily use the client-side method (which operates entirely in the Web browser, alleviating the need for a CGI at the server).

You should use moderation when you're creating pages that combine both image-mapped compositions and button schemes, lest you end up with a heavy-handed result. Resist the temptation to go overboard.

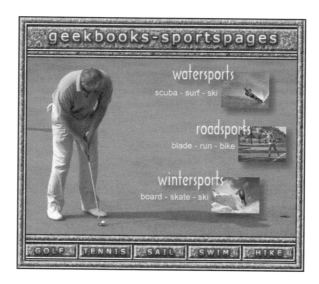

Image maps are primarily used for static images. You need to use a JavaScript rollover to make the images change when the mouse cursor passes over (say, if you want the button text to change color or glow). The next section touches on the subject of JavaScript rollovers, and Chapter 9 takes a closer look at the topic.

Designing The Interface

So what should your site's navigational structure look like? Think about the intent of your site and of the expectations of your visitors. Do your visitors already know you? If you have established a recognizable appearance in the real world, you might be wise to continue that graphic identity online. The navigational interface should ease visitors into your online world.

Flat Color Interfaces

If you value speed above all, flat color interfaces get the nod. Look at
how the portal sites such as Yahoo!, Excite, Infoseek, and Lycos deliver
their navigation. Simple text links carry the bulk of the navigational
chores. The portals can't afford to eat their bandwidth with a bunch of
graphics. The links can float freely on the page, or they can be encased in
tables with colored cell backgrounds to create unpretentious (and
speedy!) buttons.

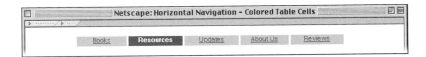

The following code creates the table. Note the cell and text color changes
in the unlinked cell (shown in gray):

```
<TABLE WIDTH="75%" BORDER="0" CELLSPACING="3" CELLPADDING="2">
<TR>
    <TD WIDTH="20%" ALIGN="CENTER" BGCOLOR="#99cccc"
    VALIGN="TOP">
        <FONT SIZE="-1" FACE="Trebuchet MS, Arial, Helvetica">
<A HREF="books.html">Books</A></FONT></TD>
    <TD WIDTH="20%" ALIGN="CENTER" BGCOLOR="#003366"
    VALIGN="TOP">
<B><FONT COLOR="#ffffff" SIZE="-1" FACE="Trebuchet, MS Arial,
Helvetica">Resources</FONT></B></TD>
    <TD WIDTH="20%" ALIGN="CENTER" BGCOLOR="#99cccc"
    VALIGN="TOP">
<FONT SIZE="-1" FACE="Trebuchet, MS Arial, Helvetica">
<A HREF="updates.html">Updates</A></FONT></TD>
    <TD WIDTH="20%" ALIGN="CENTER" BGCOLOR="#99cccc"
    VALIGN="TOP">
<A HREF="aboutus.html"><FONT SIZE="-1" FACE="Trebuchet,
MS Arial, Helvetica">About Us</FONT></A></TD>
    <TD WIDTH="20%" ALIGN="CENTER" BGCOLOR="#99cccc"
    VALIGN="TOP">
<FONT SIZE="-1" FACE="Trebuchet, MS Arial, Helvetica">
<A HREF="reviews.html">Reviews</A></FONT></TD>
</TR>
</TABLE>
```

With this approach, the status of the currently selected section would be
reflected on the button bar of each page. Colored table cells are the fastest
way to create highlighted buttons.

3D Interfaces

If you seek to deliver an experience along with your information, you'll
likely hear the siren song of the 3D interface. Somewhere along the way,

interactive designers decided that on-screen presentations should not mimic the printed page; they should emulate the tactile world instead. Although magazines and newspapers are not commonly designed with a 3D look, the practice has become commonplace on the Web. There, 3D interfaces often use beveled, embossed, or floating buttons, as shown in the following figure.

Designers used to have to rely on their Adobe Photoshop skills (and plug-ins) to create snazzy 3D buttons. Newer programs, such as Adobe ImageStyler and Macromedia Fireworks, have made 3D button creation a point-and-shoot affair.

Rollover And Bark!

Interactive navigational buttons have become quite popular. Using JavaScript, you can show a different image when the cursor is over the image area, and a third image when the mouse is clicked. These states are referred to as *MouseOver* or *rollover* states. The following illustration shows a combination of **noAction**, **onMouseOver**, and **onMouseDown** states. Initially, the **noAction** image is displayed. As the cursor touches the button, the text glows (**onMouseOver**). When the button is clicked, the button appears as if it has been pressed (**onMouseDown**).

You can create the rollover actions in a number of ways, in addition to writing your own JavaScript or adapting scripts you find on the Web. Web page layout packages such as Adobe GoLive and Macromedia Dreamweaver include the rollover creation capabilities, as do the companies' respective Web graphics tools (ImageStyler and Fireworks).

Picking A Metaphor (Or Not)

Some sites fall into the trap of using metaphors as links. Be careful; using metaphors correctly and effectively is not easy. What may be obvious to you may be alien to your visitors. You should never assume that they will get it. Try not to get (too) cute. Although playful is okay, obscurity is not. The old adage "Say what you mean, and mean what you say" applies.

Using Icons

The original premise behind the use of icons was that an icon could tell more with a picture than could be told with words, given the same amount of space. That's the premise, although as it has turned out, it's not always the practice. Nowadays, icons are often used with explanatory text to increase the level of comprehension.

Designing With Frames

Frames afford the Web page designer the ability to create modular Web sites with a persistent structure. In this way, you can create a flexible site, where certain items such as headers, advertising banners, and navigational devices remain intact as your visitors scroll about through the content and jump from page to page. This modular persistency can benefit your Web site in a number of ways:

- Logos and other ID graphics get more face time.

- Static advertising banners enhance the probability that the visitors will actually read the banner and, as the advertiser would hope, click through.

- Consistent navigation can benefit the user interface.

How Do Frames Work?

In short, framed Web pages are nothing more than simple containers for other Web pages. Perhaps, thinking of a framed layout as a little curio cabinet might help. You're allowed to build as many "shelves" as you want (although common sense says to never exceed four—use more and you'll be on thin Net ice) in your cabinet, although each shelf (frame) is capable of holding just one item at a time. The curio cabinet is known as a *frameset,* with each shelf holding an individual Web page. When you click a link on a framed page, the new page is displayed within the *targeted* window. You specify the target window when you create your links.

The frameset is a rather terse little file, basically consisting of a page title, along with references to the initial frame source files, as well as sizing, naming, and scrolling information. When you're referring to the URL of a framed Web site, always refer to the URL of the frameset, not of the frames contained therein.

Here's an example of a simple two-frame frameset with a left site navigational frame, along with the frameset code:

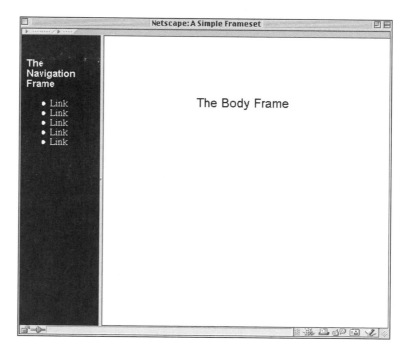

```
<HTML>
<HEAD>
  <TITLE>A Simple Frameset</TITLE>
</HEAD>
<FRAMESET FRAMEBORDER=1 COLS="22%,78%">
<FRAME SRC="left-nav.html" NAME="navigation">
<FRAME SRC="body.html" NAME="body">
<NOFRAMES>
<BODY>
```

```
Insert the no frames message here!
</BODY>
</NOFRAMES>
</FRAMESET>
</HTML>
```

How Many Frames?

So, you think you want to carve up your design into frames? Consider this move carefully; poorly implemented frames can ruin your visitors' experience. Always keep simplicity at the forefront of your designs. In practice, the most effective framed Web sites use either a two-, three-, or four-frame layout. Let's take a look at some basic examples of each layout.

Two Frames

Do you just want to keep your navigational structure separate from the content of your pages? By using a simple two-frame layout, you can stuff the navigation and site identification into a top, side, or bottom frame. This solution can be clean and elegant. A two-frame layout is often the least obtrusive design.

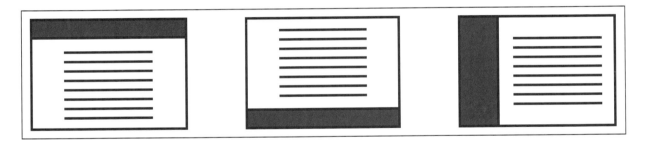

Three Frames

Need to accommodate two persistent elements? A three-frame layout can handle navigation and advertising in separate frames. Three frames provide a wide degree of flexibility.

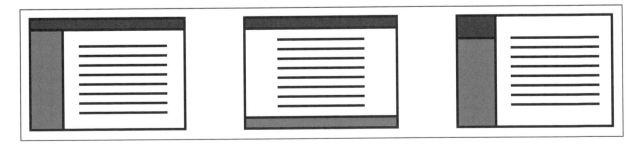

Four Frames

Into complexity? If you execute your four-framed layout carefully, you can deliver your message effectively. Miss your mark, however, and you'll send your visitors into a rage. With four frames, the layout can start to get cluttered.

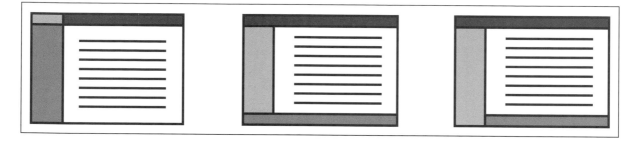

Think About Color

If you're considering a four- (or more) frame layout bcause of the volume of information you need to present, you should pay extra heed to the background color of each frame that you plan to use. You can reduce the visual complexity of the interface by using the same background color for two adjoining frames. This solution can be especially effective when used with nonbordered, nonscrolling frames.

Frame Options

Frames provide a number of important design options, including the following:

- *Frame Border*—Can be set to bordered or borderless.

- *Height*—Can be set for horizontal frames in percentage, pixel, or relative terms.

- *Width*—Can be set for vertical frames in percentage, pixel, or relative terms.

- *Margin Width*—Can set the amount of space between the left and right sides of a frame and its contents.

- *Margin Height*—Can set the amount of space between the top and bottom sides of a frame and its contents.

- *Scrollbars*—Can be set to Yes, No, or Auto. If the frame's content doesn't require scrollbars, be sure to set this option to No.

- *Anchor At*—Can allow you to set up a framed page so that it opens at a specific point within a frame.

- *Viewer Resizable*—Can disallow resizing if you don't want visitors to resize specific windows (such as advertising banners).

Moving On

If your audience is accustomed to driving a family sedan, don't drop them into the cockpit of an F-14 jet. Give them a familiar place to play; design the navigational interface with ease of use as the primary concern. All the fancy doodads in the world won't do a bit of good if your audience can't figure out how to get from here to there. The next chapter covers the topic of site structure, as you move from creating individual Web pages into the realm of Web site design and planning.

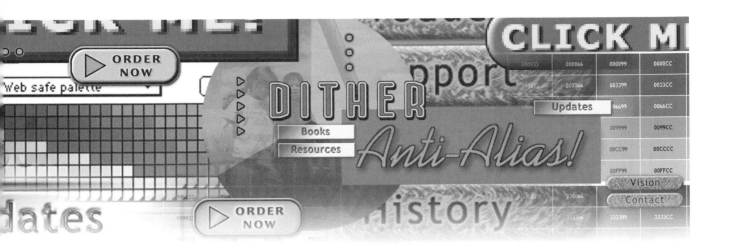

CREATING SITE STRUCTURE 8

Great Web sites are more than just an assemblage of random pages; they provide a coherent user experience.

How do you feel when you visit a neighbor's house? Does it give you a sense of ease or unease? Do you feel as if you're a welcome guest or as if you are an interloper? Your Web site is your virtual home. By envisioning it as such, you can begin to see the site from the visitors' perspective. This chapter provides strategies for the creation of user-friendly sites as it spells out a number of ways to increase warmth and effectiveness.

Envisioning Site Structure

Get a clear vision of where you want your site to go before you begin to build the pages. Determine the scope of the site and create a list of features. This list will help you break up the site into sections and pages. Great houses (and Web sites) are built to grow to suit the needs of their inhabitants because those needs change over time. You don't have to build everything at once; just make sure that you leave room for expansion.

Cabin, Mansion, Or Palace

So, how do you picture your Web site? Is it a cabin, a mansion, or a palace? It helps to think of the process of laying out the pages as similar to the research that an architect does when sitting down with clients to design a custom home. Walk through your online home, and envision the passageways from room to room. The static navigational system should provide a standard way to get from one page to the next. Links within the page content allow your visitors to jump from page to page in context.

Over time, many of your pages will be accessed directly as a result of search engine queries. You must be prepared for your visitors to show up in any room of your house—not just at the front door. After your visitors arrive, the site must be immediately navigable. Your visitors must be able to quickly find what they need.

The Cocktail Napkin

I don't know how many times I've written or said this, but it's worth repeating again: Sketch out your plans on paper before you commit them to the screen. By sketching out the site structure on paper, you can take it everywhere you go; you're not tied to your desk or to your computer. Inspiration can strike anywhere from the kitchen table to the hammock to the morning train ride to the boardroom. You might carry a notebook computer on business trips, but it's far easier to pull out a pad of paper on the taxi ride from the airport to the hotel.

Don't the best ideas happen on a cocktail napkin?

Tying It Together

As visitors move from room to room (page to page), they should always feel that they are in the same house (site). Although making minor decorative changes is okay, page style and structure should not change abruptly. You should maintain the same type sizes, type styles, and layout dimensions. A consistent background and color scheme are highly recommended. Although the page content will change, the basic container should not. Great sites flow seamlessly from one page to the next.

The Front Page

Think of the face that your home turns to the street. The facade of your Web site needs to be inviting and familiar to welcome your visitors. Like people in the real estate business say, "First impressions count." If the front door of your site is nicely turned out, your visitors will be more likely to come inside and have a look around. If the place looks like a dump, they'll drive right on by.

Making a good first impression is more than just looking good. The front page needs to deliver an enticing taste of the site contents. You need to leave enough tasty appetizers on the front porch to lure them deeper into the house you built.

The Splash Page

In certain instances, your front page might take the form of a *splash page*. A splash page serves as an introduction to the site. It makes a big branding statement before the visitors get to the real goods. Depending on how the splash page is implemented, it can be anything from throwaway fluff to technological exercises to essential components. You might think of the splash page as the opening riff of a song. This riff can affect the mood or expectations of the visitors. Play the wrong riff, and it will feel gratuitous. Play it right, and you'll prime your visitors for what lies ahead.

Splash pages are not essential—save for one key situation. The search engines have a difficult time dealing with framed sites; their ranking always suffers. A nonframed splash page presents more palatable spider bait to the search engine crawlers. Framed sites should always make use of a clear, concise, well-structured (nonframed) splash page, laden with good content.

Some Web site designers take the concept of splash pages to another level. They create special splash pages, known as *doorway pages*, for each of the major search engines—Inktomi, AltaVista, Excite, Lycos, and Infoseek—

that are fine-tuned to provide the highest ranking. Each of the search engines uses different criteria to rank a page, based on the search terms. If you tweak each doorway page to suit the criteria of a specific engine, the page can achieve the best possible rank. All of the doorway pages are not submitted to every search engine; each engine receives only the version fine-tuned for its tastes. Therefore, the AltaVista-tuned page is submitted only to AltaVista, the Inktomi-tuned page is submitted only to Inktomi (via **www.hotbot.com**), and so on.

The Table Of Contents

Open any magazine, and flip through the first pages. After you pass the obligatory full-page advertisements, you soon arrive at the table of contents. Although the cover of the magazine may offer a few tantalizing tidbits along with a juicy photograph, the table of contents really sets readers headed off in the right direction. This same dynamic element works also on the Web as well. If the splash page is the face that your Web site puts to the street, the table of contents is the grand foyer, with direct passageways to the most important rooms inside. In it, you will need to include lead-ins to topics and pointers to pages.

The table of contents should be a constantly evolving page that reflects what's happening on your site at that precise moment in time. Consider it a showcase of not only what's hot, but also what's most important.

The Rooms

Now, think about the rooms inside your house. Through convention, society has come up with standards: the living room, the kitchen, the dining room, the bedrooms, and the bathroom. Web sites are much the same way; your visitors will expect to find things in the same familiar places. Make it easy for them to find what they're looking for. If they expect to find something in the bathroom, don't hide it in the kitchen.

- Let your visitors know how to get in touch. Provide contact information with full details (phone, fax, email, and snail mail address).

- Let them know what's happening. Provide information on what's new with the site and with your company.

- Let them know who you are. Provide company details, such as press releases, corporate history, officers, board members (if public), and links to press coverage.

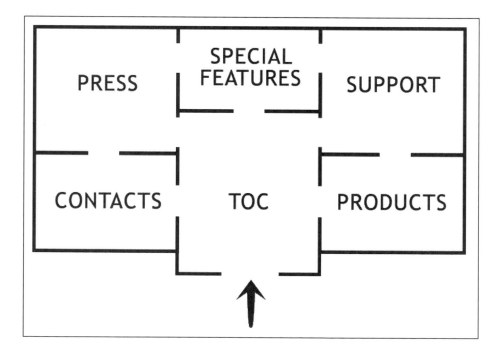

Assessing Roadblocks, Avoiding Detours

The site structure should make each page accessible through a number of avenues. Never give your guests just one way to find a page. As the site grows, you should provide two additional means to navigate the site: a site map and a search facility. The site map and search function should be accessible from each and every page.

Play Cards

When you begin to arrange your Web site into sections, you'll likely run into situations in which placing a page is difficult. Earlier, I suggested that you might sketch out your site before committing a pixel. Now, I want to suggest that you take things one step further by turning this organizational process into a little table game. Get a stack of index cards (or cut up some paper into little squares). Write a page name on each card. Find a nice big table to spread out all the cards. Try organizing the cards in different hierarchical patterns, and imagine yourself walking through the links to get a feel for the flow that your site should take.

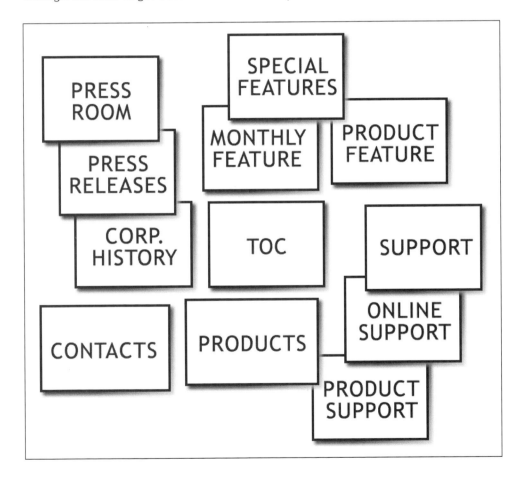

Minimize the number of steps required to get from the front door to the hottest topics. Avoid burying any page too deeply in the structure. When the arrangement feels right, turn the card layout into a written hierarchical chart—before a stiff breeze blows through the window!

Create A Site Map

The site map is the place where folks come to when they get lost. The site map should allow guests to find their way around your site by delivering the hierarchy of pages in a clean and concise manner. Don't make it an overly cute, metaphor-laden page. Give folks what they need, and send them on their way.

Have you ever found yourself in the lobby of a large office building or skyscraper? Every lobby includes a building directory to help visitors find their way. The site map serves the same purpose. The bigger the Web site, the greater the importance of the site map. A 6-page site doesn't need a site map, a 60-page site is a likely candidate, and a 600-page site should never do without.

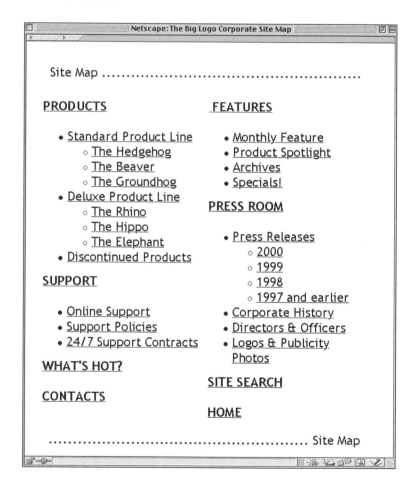

Provide A Search Facility

A search facility is one of the friendliest and most productive utilities that you can add to your site. Not only does it help your visitors find exactly what they are looking for, it can also provide you with valuable data.

A server-based search engine should produce a log of search term entries. As a result, you can see, at a glance, what the majority of visitors are looking for. (See Chapter 11 fo a cool search engine service.)

Open A Line Of Dialog

What prevents your visitors from finding what they need? You won't know until you ask. After your Web site is online, it should provide an open line of dialog with its guests. Give visitors the opportunity to send feedback—either through a simple email link or through a mail form. You should answer all inquiries promptly, first with an autoresponder, followed shortly by real human contact. The incoming email should be cataloged in a database; cataloging helps in the assessment of site issues based on the volume of mail.

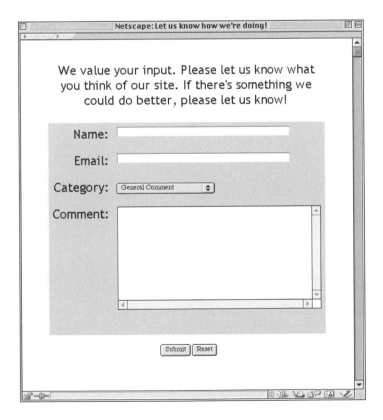

Some folks will be happy to provide feedback; they just want to be heard. Others visitors may need a little incentive—in the form of a freebie or giveaway—to liberate their opinions.

Other forms of dialog may include the following:

- Instant polls

- Questionnaires

- User forums

Measuring Success

Every Web site will have a different barometer of success. We all seek a busy site, although success can never be measured by sheer traffic alone. A stampede of visitors who have little interest in what you need them to be interested in is just a waste of bandwidth. To be successful, you must set your goals, watch your traffic patterns, and adjust your site accordingly.

Setting Goals

Set realistic goals for your site, and then measure your success against these goals on a regular basis. With Internet usage still on the upswing, you should set results a little higher each period. Growth is the name of the game. At the end of each period, ask the appropriate questions:

- Did the site produce more inquiries?

- Did the site generate more subscribers?

- Did the site sell more advertising space?

- Did the site sell more goods?

- Did the site generate more income through its affiliate links?

If the site hasn't grown, figure out why. Put steps in place to grow the site, and then raise your goals. Don't become complacent. Keep raising the bar.

ANALYZE THIS!

Here's a pair of popular server-log analysis tools:

Sawmill

www.flowerfire.com/

WebTrends

www.webtrends.com

Watching Traffic

Savvy Webmasters watch their site traffic to see the road their visitors are taking on the way to their sites, where they first enter the site, and on which page they end up. Every Web server request generates a line of data containing information about the client, as well as the referring and requested page. This data is compiled into the server log file. The server log file can look like a bunch of gibberish to the neophyte. It's best to use a server-log analysis tool to develop site statistics and determine traffic trends.

Moving On

I cannot overemphasize the importance of site structure and its impact on the user experience. You should treat your guests like guests. Extend them welcome, see to their needs, provide what they seek, and be the best host you can possibly be. The next chapter delves into interactivity, with an overview of animation, JavaScript, audio, video, and other cool technologies.

ADDING
INTERACTIVITY

9

A static Web site gets you only so far. Sometimes, you need to go for the flash and sizzle.

Does your Web site just sit there? Do you long for a captivating interactive experience that enthralls the visitors and wows your boss? If so, it might be time to take a walk on the wild side and add some action to your site. This chapter provides an overview of the most popular technologies for adding movement, interactivity and multimedia elements, as it explains how GIF animations, JavaScript, Java applets, Shockwave, QuickTime, RealVideo, and sound files can bring newfound life to your site. Use these tools sparingly. Although interactive features can take a static site to new levels, the wise Web designer wields this power with discretion.

Interactivity Built Into The Browser

Let's take a quick look back at the progression of Web design. In the beginning, there were plain old hypertext pages. Graphics were soon added to the equation, in the form of GIF and JPEG files. These early text and graphic pages delivered the functional equivalent of a newspaper page. You could read the news, and you could see the pictures, but nothing jumped off the page. You could click on (what looked like) a button, and you would be whisked away to another location. Something was missing.

As the browsers evolved early on, provisions for movement and interactivity were added. The introduction of GIF animation capabilities in Netscape Navigator 2 changed the way Web pages behaved. With GIF animation, images could move and dance. Netscape also introduced Web page scripting to the world in Navigator 2. What we now know as JavaScript was initially called LiveScript (Netscape renamed it to hook into the Java buzz). With the introduction of this exciting technology, Web pages entered the realm of true interactivity.

GIF Animation

If you're looking for an inexpensive, fast, and simple way to get your Web site hopping, look no further. GIF89a animations can bring movement to your site without costing you much time, cash, or bandwidth. You can easily implement them: Just place them into your pages as you would any other GIF image.

Animated GIFs have been around (at least in terms of the Internet) for some time now. When GIF89a animation hit the Web in late 1995, one of the first places it came into vogue was on advertising banners. Ad agency Web designers quickly discovered that they could use GIF animations to accomplish design tricks previously reserved for broadcast graphics.

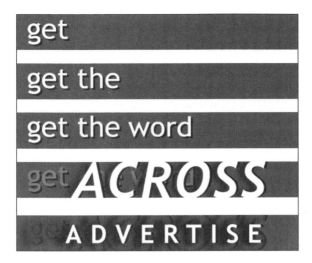

GIF89a animations are created when the browser displays a series of *cels* (or frames—think of a strip of film) in sequence. These cels can consist of images, text, or a combination of both elements. GIF animations must be kept to a small file size to download and render quickly. One of the best ways to learn about animated GIFs is to cruise the Web in search of some good examples. The Appendix includes a short list of some of the coolest animation Web sites, as well as a number of GIF animation tools.

GIF animation can be fun, but the wrong animations can quickly send your site design on a one-way ticket to Cheezyland. Have you ever landed on a page that was so overloaded with tacky animation that you ran out of the room with a case of motion sickness? Imprudent use (or overuse) of animation is a hallmark of the novice Web designer.

JavaScript

Although GIF animation added movement to Web pages, it was Netscape's other innovation in Navigator 2.0 that made the most difference in interactivity. The addition of JavaScript allowed for a high degree of interaction. Whereas GIF animation may add motion to a page, it does not interact with the user. GIF animation just *plays,* JavaScript *interacts.* Chapter 7 touched on some of the capabilities of JavaScript, with brief discussions of pop-up navigational menus and rollover buttons, but the capabilities go far past those two parlor tricks. The possibilities afforded by JavaScript are endless.

Before JavaScript, Web designers had to rely on CGI scripts at the server to work with Web page forms. JavaScript said, "Hey, you don't need to have a dumb form now that you have an able browser." When developers built JavaScript ability into the browser, it became possible to perform computations locally rather than across the Web. Scripts sprung forth to provide every possible type of function; things began to happen at the Web browser that were previously found only in resident applications.

JavaScript is a relatively straightforward scripting language. It's not as complex nor as powerful as programming languages such as C or Java. So, what can JavaScript do for you? Here are some examples:

- *Alert messages*—Pop up an alert box to grab your visitors' attention.

- *Browser detection*—Get the goods on your visitors' browsers. The browsers will cough up an array of details, including the name of the browser, version number, client IP address, referring page, screen size, and resident plug-ins, among others. These details can be used to redirect the client to a browser-specific page.

- *Calculators*—Blast through your math problems with everything from simple calculators through mortgage amortization and scientific functions.

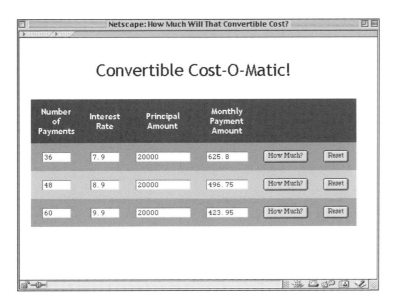

- *Clocks and calendars*—Place the current time and date on a page or provide time-based calculations.

- *Form validation*—Check a form for completeness *before* it's sent to the server. Validating forms at this point saves time and ensures the cleanest data.

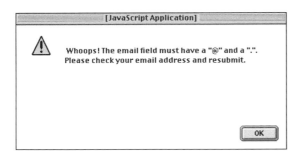

- *Scrolling text*—Put text in motion. Text can move with variations from classic horizontal tickers to vertical scrolls.

LATEST NEWS	LATEST NEWS	LATEST NEWS
DATELINE - WASHINGTON: The President is embroiled with yet another scandal, this time involving the First Dog. It seems that the First Lady has insisted that the President walk the First Dog each night before bedtime.	each night before bedtime. The President had other plans. By handing over the duties to one of his most trusted aides, the President has forsaken the trust between	forsaken the trust between a man and his dog. "I can't believe how lazy he is!" said the House Majority Leader. "What kind of man can't take the time to walk his own dog?"

- *Rollovers*—Make navigational buttons come to life, with this most common of all JavaScripts. The buttons appear to depress (or perform some other high jinks) when you click on them.

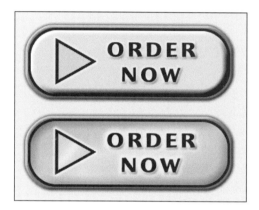

- *Rotate ad banners*—Keep pages from getting stale by rotating your advertising banners.

And, that's just the start!

Although JavaScript is powerful, it does have a few operational problems that you need to consider. The thorniest issue when working with JavaScript is an inconsistency of support between the different Netscape and Microsoft Web browsers. A script that runs flawlessly on one browser may break in the next. The script can get snagged in many places. The inability of Microsoft Internet Explorer 3 to display rollovers, for example, is one of the most common snags. If you plan on including JavaScript in your pages, you would be well advised to check the pages from all of the major Web browsers and OS platforms.

DHTML

Dynamic HTML (DHTML) is a progression of JavaScript. First found in the version 4 browsers, DHTML allows JavaScript to take charge of Document Object Model (DOM) elements. Dynamic documents can react to a wide range of criteria, including time, browser, and user input. DHTML was a darling of both the cutting-edge Web design crowd and software developers who rushed to provide Web page tools that delivered this functionality. Hype aside, it's prudent to wait until you master the basics of Web design before you begin to incorporate DHTML into your Web pages.

Java

Java was originally developed by Sun Microsystems, with the intent of creating a totally cross-platform programming language. The dream was "write once, run anywhere." Java applets are little programs that are downloaded along with a Web page. The Web page coding usually contains parameters that control how the applets behave. As a Web site developer, you probably won't deal with the actual programming involved in creating a Java applet. In many cases, you'll either use a prebuilt applet or have an engineer create an applet specifically for the application at hand. It's important, however, that your applet runs in a cross-platform environment.

Interactivity Through Plug-Ins And Helpers

Although the capability to include GIF animation, JavaScript, DHTML, and Java is built into the newer Web browsers, a whole slew of interactivity and multimedia elements requires browser plug-ins or helper applications. Technologies such as Shockwave, Flash, QuickTime, RealAudio, and RealVideo demand that your visitors properly outfit and configure their browsers to fully experience your multimedia masterpiece. If they don't have the plug-ins loaded, they miss out on all the tasty stuff.

Macromedia Shockwave

Macromedia's Shockwave first rumbled through the Web in late 1996. The technology raised quite a stir in the Web community by bringing the power of Macromedia Director and the creativity of its massive user base (well over 250,000 users) to the Internet. Director is the most prevalent tool in the multimedia industry, and Macromedia boasts some of the most talented third-party developers in the world.

Shockwave adds an enhanced level of interactivity to Web pages. The Shockwave plug-in has proven to be one of the most popular on the Internet; Macromedia boasts that its site has served up millions upon millions of copies of the installation files. When you incorporate native Shockwave into your Web site, you are taking a leap of faith; you're betting that your visitors will have Shockwave installed or that they will be sufficiently intrigued to download and install the plug-in. Thankfully, Shockwave has been bundled with Netscape Navigator and Microsoft Internet Explorer for some time now.

Macromedia started out by creating Shockwave files from Director, its flagship multimedia application. The company soon added versions for FreeHand (vector graphics), Authorware (computer-based training), and xRes (high-end bitmaps)—although all but the Director version have fallen off the "hypescope." The most dramatic addition, however, was Macromedia Flash, which brought interactive vector animations into the loop.

Macromedia Flash

Macromedia Flash changed the game in Web page animation, as its big brother Director did before it. Flash actually began life as FutureSplash Animator. Macromedia acquired FutureSplash in early 1997 and quickly relaunched Animator as Flash. Unlike most techniques that are based on bitmap animation, Flash uses vector animation. This capability allows for smaller files that download more quickly. Synchronized sound is supported in the form of WAV and AIFF files. This capability allows for everything from simple button noises through more complex arrangements.

You might think of the difference between Macromedia Director and Flash as the difference between Adobe Photoshop and Illustrator. Director and Photoshop both deal with bitmaps. Flash and Illustrator both deal with vector art (although they can incorporate bitmaps). Whereas one provides its images in bit-by-bit detail, the other delivers its images with bold, object-oriented graphics. Today, Director is used more for online games, whereas Flash is used for immersive interfaces and engaging *interstitials*. (Intersitials are often used as advertising that runs in-between, rather than inside of, Web pages.)

Audio

Nothing sets the mood like a good soundtrack and some carefully chosen sound effects. You can add a soundtrack to a page by using the <EMBED> tag and implement button click sounds within a JavaScript rollover. Sound files generally have one of the following extensions: .AIF, .AIFF, .AU, .WAV, .MP3, .MID, or .MIDI. Apple's QuickTime is widely used for sound and music, as well.

For your visitors to hear sounds on your Web pages, their computers must be set up with the appropriate hardware and software. Whereas all Macintosh computers have the built-in hardware capability to play analog sounds (AIF, AIFF, AU, and WAV), Windows computers are not always equipped with sound cards. The browser must be properly configured to hear sound files as well.

AU, AIFF, And WAV Files

You need the appropriate software to create your own sound files. Fortunately, you don't have to spend a dime to get started. If you're working on a Macintosh, you can use the Mac's Sound Control Panel to record. Then, you can use SoundApp (a cool little freeware program) to convert it to the appropriate format. If you're working with a Windows computer, you can use the built-in Windows Sound Recorder to create and save the file. The AU and AIFF formats are the best choices for cross-platform playback; therefore, you may want to convert any WAV files before incorporating them into your Web pages.

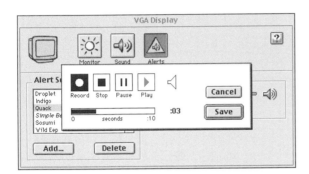

Of course, as your needs and expectations increase, you'll want to edit and enhance your recordings. Fortunately, a host of shareware sound applications is available. You can find a list of Internet sound resources in the Appendix.

MIDI Files

MIDI files are different from the other formats in two important ways. You can think of them as digital sheet music in a way. MIDI files are programs that provide instructions on how a song will play. Analog sound files are recordings, in the same vein as tape recordings. Also, MIDI files may require an additional plug-in to play at the browser.

RealAudio

RealAudio is a *streaming* media format. It differs from the AIF, AIFF, AU, MP3, and WAV formats in that the RealAudio files begin playing before the entire file is downloaded from the server. When the first part of a RealAudio file reaches the browser, the file begins to play, as the remainder of the file streams down from the server. The use of RealAudio depends on two key elements: The files must be served from a Real Server, and the RealAudio Player must be installed at the client side (your visitors' computers).

WHAT ABOUT MP3?

The MP3 (MPEG Layer 3) format has quickly become the digital music format of choice, due to its high levels of compression and quality. Although MP3 is popular for high-end music applications, the files are generally too large to use as Web page soundtracks.

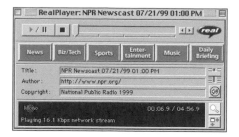

Video

Want to put some real moving pictures on your Web site? I can't think of a cooler way than using digital video. Although you have to get used to the chunky images, Net-based video is a harbinger of what's to come—thousands of micro-broadcasters, beaming their programming around the world, not through the airways, but over the Web.

QuickTime

Apple's QuickTime is one of the most popular methods to deliver video clips via the Web. The medium allows you to show everything from your Frisbee-catching family dog to your latest whizzy invention in glorious full motion. And, these movies work great in cross-platform situations; the QuickTime plug-in is one of most prevalent on the Web—having shipped with millions upon millions of browsers. The latest version, QuickTime 4, is a streaming media format, similar in intent to RealVideo, although QuickTime 4 one ups RealVideo by providing support for Macromedia Flash.

You can place QuickTime movies into your Web pages by using the **<EM-BED>** command. Movies are typically quite large because they usually contain both sound and video (although QuickTime is becoming an increasingly popular format for sound files). Adding a QuickTime clip to a Web page is a powerful way to convey information, but if the QuickTime movie is huge, you should always make it an optional choice for your visitors. Put the clip on a separate page, and make sure the link to that page includes a polite warning about the file size. In other words, don't put a 4MB file on the front page of your Web site.

WHAT ABOUT AVI?

QuickTime gets the nod over the competing AVI movie format because QuickTime is more widely supported. The bottom line: If you're considering adding movies to your Web site, QuickTime's the best way to go (unless you're ready to invest in a Real Server).

RealVideo

RealVideo is a streaming media format, like RealAudio and QuickTime 4.
RealVideo typically plays in the RealPlayer, rather than in the browser,
and must be served from a Real Server.

Moving On

In this chapter, you learned about various methods to bring action,
interactivity, and a multimedia experience to your Web site. Because
the line between sizzle and sludge can be fine, resist the temptation
to go overboard with fancy add-ons that add little to the value of your
content. Add value, not gadgets. The next chapter provides an overview
of Web advertising.

DESIGNING WEB ADVERTISING

10

Buying Web advertising is like playing the horses. Do your homework, bet wisely, cross your fingers, and you just might end up in the winner's circle.

The sad truth about most Internet advertising is that it's an extreme long shot. A 100-to-1 horse breaking out of an outside gate has a better chance of finishing in the money. Most Web surfers have learned to filter out advertising banners: They don't see them, they don't click on them, they don't even remember seeing such banners. For a banner to earn a click, it has to do something different. To be effective, the banner must reach out and grab the viewers by the collar, slap them across both cheeks, and scream at them, "Hey, you! Look at me!" Although the banner needn't be harsh, it must speak directly to the needs or desires of the viewers. Highly targeted advertising campaigns make the most sense; banners need to preach to the converted, not to the masses.

Hey You ... *Click Here* **NOW!**

Think about all the banners you've seen in the last week. Now, think about the banners you clicked on. Which banners (if any) earned your attention? Have you *ever* purchased anything as a result of clicking on a banner? Many folks haven't; it's a huge issue. The Internet advertising business continues to struggle to deliver adequate bang for the advertiser's buck. Well-managed advertising campaigns deliver eager customers to merchants ready and willing to make the deal.

Forms Of Web Advertising

Web advertising comes in many varieties, not just banner ads. The following sections help you identify the most prevalent types of Web advertising.

Banner Advertising

Conventional banner advertising uses a model borrowed from the print world. It resembles newspaper or magazine advertising in which a fraction of the page is sold to the advertiser. As with a newspaper page, Web publishers can pack a number of advertisements onto one page by using different sizes of ad banners and buttons. (You can find a table of common banner ad sizes toward the end of this chapter.) Of course, the more advertisements you pack on a page, the more you lower the potential return for each advertisement.

Banner advertising is typically sold via one of three methods:

- Cost Per Thousand Impressions (CPM)—The advertiser pays a flat fee for each thousand impressions of the banner. If the CPM rate is $40, and the advertiser purchases 10,000 impressions, the advertising campaign costs a fixed $400.

- Per Click—The advertiser pays each time someone clicks on a banner. (This method is often referred to as click-through.) If the click-through rate is $.10 and the banner is clicked on 400 times, the campaign costs the advertiser $40. If that same banner is clicked on only 200 times, the campaign costs $20.

- Revenue Sharing—The advertiser pays a percentage of sales resulting from click-throughs. If $1,000 worth of goods or services is purchased and the commission rate is 15 percent, the advertiser pays $150. If $2,000 worth of goods or services is purchased and the commission rate is 10 percent, the advertiser pays $200. If no goods are sold, the advertiser owes nothing. All of the impressions are free.

Notice the great deal of difference in these schemes. The ultimate benefit to each of the parties depends on the accuracy of ad placement. The CPM model is based purely on the number of times the banner ad is displayed. The per-click and revenue-sharing models are based on an event or an event sequence—either a simple click-through or a click-through and purchase—to trigger payment.

When purchasing advertising via the CPM method, the advertiser can burn cash and produce absolutely no result. Although the per-click model can be a cost-effective method, it's the revenue sharing model that really makes Web publishers work for their fees. Revenue sharing (most often referred to as *associate* or *affiliate marketing*) is the most equitable method of all; both the advertiser and publisher can profit handsomely.

Interstitial Advertising

Let's pause for a word from our sponsor! The concept of *interstitial advertising* was that the advertisement would interrupt the surfers' flow by displaying itself between an editorial click-through and the summoned page—much in the same way that a radio or television commercial interrupts your regularly scheduled program. (Interstitial advertisements are set apart from the regular content, rather than placed within the page.) You might also think of it as being akin to a full-page advertisement appearing between editorial pages in a magazine article. More than just static ads, interstitials promised to deliver television-like commercials, with an interactive hook. Although the concept was pretty cool, interstitials never really took off, due to bandwidth limitations; 56K modems were just not fast enough to support serious video.

Pop-Up Windows

The high-end interstitial concept morphed into the annoying low-end pop-up ad window commonly found on a number of community sites. Contests and other special marketing campaigns can use pop-ups to great effect. When visitors hit an active sports-oriented Web site, for example, they are more likely to be interested in a contest that offers a mountain bike as a prize rather than a canned ham. The pop-up should offer some perceived value to the visitors, lest it be more irritating than effective. (An ad banner alone does not justify using a pop-up.)

Sponsored Content

If I were to place a bet where the future lies in Internet advertising, I would have to plunk down my money on a variation of the sponsored content theme. In the classic days of media, upstanding publications upheld the separation of church and state. In this case, the term does not refer to religious freedom; it refers to the fine line that runs between the editorial and advertising departments. The Internet revolution kicked dirt all over that line.

The Web is full of sponsored content in the form of affiliate and associate programs. Take a look at the front page of any of the portals; you'll see lots of text links to merchant Web sites. Those unassuming text links are revenue generators; when visitors click through and make purchases, the portal receives a percentage of the sales. The shrewdest part of the deal is the sheer number of text links that can be contained on a page. Dozens of revenue-generating links can be packed into the same space that would be eaten by one advertising banner.

The concept of sponsored content began with grand schemes of Web soap operas. These days, anyone can create a sponsored site, through the means of affiliate links. Unfortunately, most folks don't take the time or expend the effort to create affiliate sites with real purpose.

Defining Goals

Let's go back to the horse races. When a two-year-old horse is entered into its first race, the horse's trainer takes a chance and places the colt or filly into a field filled with peers—other two-year-old horses. The more races the horse runs, the more the trainer learns about the horse and how it reacts to the racing environment. As the horse gains experience with each race, the trainer can study the data and determine which races to enter next. You can't expect to meet your goals if you haven't defined them. But, you can't define your goals without having some type of data on which to base your assumptions. Successful Internet advertising requires educated guesswork, followed by projections based on past performance.

Web advertising success is measured with two important criteria: click-through and click-through-to-sales.

Click-Through

What makes visitors click? That's the answer everyone wants to know. The following is some commonly (and not so commonly) accepted advice:

- *Site placement*—If you want your advertising to achieve the highest click-through levels, you must place your ad banners on the right Web sites. If you're marketing a niche product, you must buy your way into the right niches. Scour the Web for the hottest potential sites for your product.

- *Page placement*—Put the ads where folks can see them. For example, 468×60 banners are typically found at the top of the page so that folks see them first. Although you shouldn't bury banners or buttons too far down the page, you should consider repeating the top-of-page 468×60 banner at the bottom of the page as well; this technique can raise the banner's click-through ratio.

- *Compelling offer*—The offer must be attractive. The visitors must have a compelling reason to click through. Always put yourself on the other side of the Net connection. If *you* were a potential customer, would *you* be interested in the offer?

- *Call to action*—Use an impending event to hasten the visitors' urgency. Consider using terms such as "special offer good until (*date*)," "valid only until (*date*)," or everyone's favorite "Order before midnight to-night and receive *XYZ* as a special gift!"

- *Click here*—Include these essential words to give the clueless a clue. Of course, a banner still needs more than just these two would-be magi-cal words to be effective. Give your visitors a *reason* to click here.

- *Keep your banners fresh*—Don't subject folks to the same old stale ban-ner week after week. The banner's effectiveness will diminish over time. Don't be afraid to retire a banner and replace it with "fresh blood" after two or three weeks.

- *Experiment*—Direct marketing is a never-ending investigation into what works and what doesn't. Use a series of different designs and offers. Serve your visitors with banner rotation scripts.

Now, you're rounding the corner for home. Is your site going to make it to the wire or stumble in the stretch?

Click-Through-To-Sales

When potential customers click on one of your banners, where do they end up? If you want them to buy a product, the click-through must deliver them to a page where they can learn more about the product and place an order. In addition, that page should welcome them to your site, tell them who you are, and stress why they should buy that product. The ad banner should prime them; the page they land on should close the sale.

Of course, lots of folks won't be ready to buy *at that moment in time.* You need a way to stay in contact with them. If you can obtain contact information from them, you stand a good chance of making the sale with a follow-up email or a subsequent special offer.

A witty, mysterious, or seductive banner that compels the visitors to click through—without revealing the true intent of the advertiser—may achieve a high click-through rate, only to deliver a disappointing sales conversion ratio. The visitors may be merely intrigued by the banner, without having any interest in the actual offer.

The click-through-to-sales conversion ratio is the place where the rubber meets the pavement. Don't aim for a large volume of curiosity seekers. Instead, aim to deliver a focused group of informed consumers. If you've done your job by creating a targeted advertising campaign that delivers smart and willing customers, sales levels should take off.

Building Ad Banners

Although anyone can knock out a banner, not everyone can build an attractive, effective, traffic-generating advertisement. Banners can be created with a wide variety of programs—anything capable of producing a nice, tight GIF file is a likely candidate. Of course, the capabilities of certain programs will exceed others—especially when it comes to features such as special effects, file compression, and animation.

Now, take a look at some of the issues related to advertising banner dimensions, format, and file size.

Banner Dimensions

In the early days of banner advertising, banner sizes were not standardized. Web sites were free to create their own banner dimensions. This lack of standardization led to bedlam because banners designed for one site would not fit the next site's specifications. Banner designers were forced to create an infinite number of variations of each banner to suit the sites. This situation was rectified when the Internet Advertising Bureau (IAB) and the Coalition for Advertising Supported Information and Entertainment (CASIE) jointly developed a set of voluntary standards for advertising banners. The IAB/CASIE advertising banner standards are now prevalent. Table 10.1 lists the IAB/CASIE advertising banner sizes.

IAB/CASIE standard ad banner sizes.

Ad Type	Size (in Pixels)
Full banner	468 x 60
Full banner with vertical navigation bar	392 x 72
Half banner	234 x 60
Vertical banner	120 x 240
Button 1	120 x 90
Button 2	120 x 60
Square button	125 x 125
Micro button	88 x 31

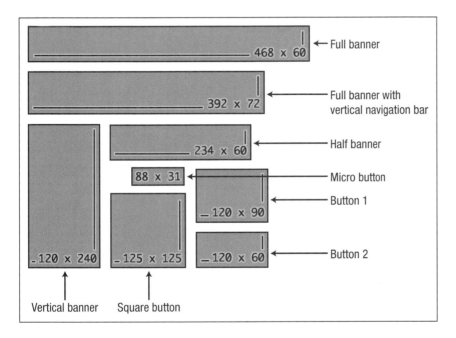

Banner Format And File Size

It's essential that ad banners load quickly and be viewable on the widest range of systems. For this reason, ad banners are generally GIF format images, with a commonly accepted maximum file size of 12K (or so). GIF banners typically use extremely limited color palettes to optimize download and display times. The tighter you make the palette, the smaller the file, the faster the download, and the sooner you get it in front of your visitors' eyes.

Your format choices are not limited to GIF. However, if you have a special banner that calls for a JPEG or Java implementation, you should check with the Web site that will be running the ad. If your banner uses a client side image map, you probably will have to supply the map HTML along with the image. You should keep alternative (**ALT**) tag text to 30 or fewer characters, as you should any linked text that runs below the banner.

Typography

Proper typeface selection is a crucial aspect of banner design, due to the extremely small amount of real estate offered by even the largest banner. The fonts you specify should work well in these harsh conditions. Although you can use both serif and sans-serif fonts, you should avoid very delicate serif designs in small type sizes; the subtle nuances do not translate well to the limited pixel environment.

Type can talk. You should use decorative fonts as an exception rather than as a rule; fancy designs often sacrifice readability for novelty. Folks should instantly understand what the banner says; they shouldn't have to spend their time scratching their heads trying to interpret that pretty type.

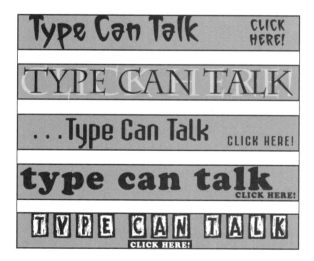

Consider using one family of typefaces on a banner—making use of regular, italic, bold, condensed, and ultra-bold variations, as appropriate. By using one type family, you stand a better chance of creating a harmonious design.

Color

The color scheme you use in your banners and buttons can have a great influence on the effectiveness of the advertisement. Stick with colors chosen from the Web-safe color palette. Brighter colors draw more attention, but you should try to avoid harsh color combinations. You want to encourage click-throughs; you don't want to blind the visitors with fluorescent colors. (Well, maybe you do.) You should provide adequate contrast between the text and background colors used in the ad. If you're going to err, don't err on the side of subtlety. Light-colored type on a dark background can be quite effective.

Photographs

Doing justice to photos in Web advertisements can be difficult. You have only so many pixels to work with! Combine diminutive banner and button size with the restrictions of the GIF format and a limited palette, and you often end up with disappointing results—smaller than postage stamp sizes, color shifts, and grainy images. Grayscale photographs can offer an interesting alternative; folks *expect* black-and-white photos to look a little grainy.

Animation

Although animation was covered in depth in Chapter 9, it's worth another mention here. Animation is popular for banner advertisements, not just because it brings movement and action, but because it allows the designer to pack more copy into the banner space. The message in an animated banner can be far more complex than the message in a static banner. Text can be staged over a sequence of frames to create a dramatic effect, heightening the impact of the message.

Moving On

Internet advertising isn't a game for the faint of heart. Someone once described the pleasure of owning a boat as having "a wooden hole in the water in which to pour money." Blindly buying banner advertising can give you that same sinking feeling, without the sea breeze. The next chapter takes a look at common design problems that can plague a Web site, as it details 20 ways to sink your ship (and make it float again).

PART III

TROUBLE-SHOOTING

CONQUERING DESIGN PROBLEMS

11

Twenty Ways To Sink Your Ship (and how to float it again).

Whether you design Web pages for fun, for charity, or for your livelihood, read on. This chapter lays out 20 ways you can upset your audience and risk your reputation as a Web designer. Of course, it also provides hints on how to avoid the heartburn. The following pages contain plenty of tips and tricks, iterating many of the topics covered elsewhere in this book. Good Web site design is about more than just cool graphics and snazzy layouts; it's about building sites that work for both the publisher and the guest.

It Breaks In The Browser

SO, WHAT CAN BREAK?

Lots of things! Often, problems can crop up with inconsistent JavaScript and CSS support between browsers. MS Internet Explorer, for example, doesn't support common JavaScript rollovers.

You can spend days designing a Web page that exploits all the coolest features in the latest version of your favorite whiz-bang browser; however, if your visitors aren't using that browser, and that page breaks, it'll take no more than a moment for them to click away (if their browsers haven't blown up, that is). If you're committed to using those whizzy tricks, include a browser-sniffing JavaScript to redirect those less-than-current browsers to an appropriately coded page.

It Requires An Obscure Plug-In

Don't make your visitors install an obscure plug-in to enjoy the content on your Web site. If you're not sure whether your plug-in of choice is prevalent, do your homework; check StatMarket (**www.statmarket.com**) to see whether the plug-in shows up on its charts. StatMarket provides a continuous source of information about what folks are *really* browsing with.

The most commonly installed plug-ins include the following:

- Adobe Acrobat PDF Viewer
- RealNetworks RealPlayer
- Macromedia Shockwave
- Macromedia Flash
- Apple QuickTime

As a courtesy, consider using a plug-in-sniffing JavaScript on the page to redirect browsers that lack the plug-in. Always include a link to the plug-in developer's Web site as well. If you want your visitors to use a specific plug-in, make it easy for them to find.

It's Too Slow

A lot of things can slow a site; the most obvious are gigantic graphics and abnormally huge HTML files. It's tough to nail down *exactly* what's too large. Without recommending a specific byte count, let me just say that you should always keep file sizes to a minimum. Put yourself in the role of the visitors. Test how your site performs from a variety of Internet connections—28.8 and 56K modems, ISDN and DSL lines, cable modems, and T1 lines, as well. (It's always helpful to have some buddies check out your site from their Internet connections, while measuring the download time.) What seems fine on a fast connection may be molasses over an older modem. Some Web page layout programs, such as Adobe PageMill, provide download time estimates. Pay attention to these estimates as you're building your pages. Pages should download and display in seconds, not minutes.

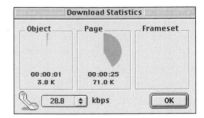

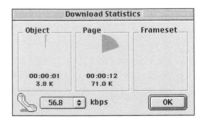

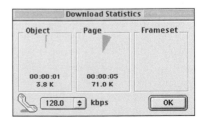

The following tips will take you a long way in the right direction for building fast Web pages:

- Don't load up on eye candy. Keep your graphics to a minimum. Try to get as much color from HTML table cell backgrounds as possible.

- Set the page background color rather than use a background image.

- Size graphics appropriately. Don't make them physically larger than they need to be; if you can make a 120×120 graphic do the work of a 240×240 image, for example, you can shave a considerable amount of time off the download.

- Crop photographs to the most important subject matter. Don't waste pixels, bytes, and seconds on superfluous imagery.

- Compress graphics as far as you can without overly affecting the image quality. Use tight palettes on GIF images, and avoid dithering, when possible. Use the highest reasonable levels of JPEG compression.

- Reuse your graphics from page to page. Doing so avoids unnecessary downloads. After a graphic file has been downloaded once, it will display instantaneously when reused on the next Web page.

- Use **WIDTH**, **HEIGHT**, and Alternate Text (**ALT**) attributes on graphics. When you use the WIDTH and HEIGHT attributes, text flows around the graphics while they are downloading. Although the *entire* page doesn't load any faster, visitors can begin reading the text instantly. Alternate Text displays before the graphic downloads. When you use **WIDTH**, **HEIGHT**, and **ALT** attributes, the IMG SRC code might look something like the following example of code:

```
<IMG SRC="hotsauce.gif" WIDTH="153" HEIGHT="30" ALT="Hot
Sauce!">
```

- Break big layout tables into several smaller tables. Large layout tables that contain many graphics can take a long time to download and display—and all this time, your visitors are staring at a blank Web page. If you chop the large table into smaller contiguous tables, individual elements are displayed more rapidly.

The Color Shifts

Design your GIF graphics so that the largest contiguous areas of flat color use colors chosen from the Web-safe palette. Doing so avoids dithering and color shifts in the most noticeable areas. Double-check your pages from a variety of displays (256 color, thousands of colors, and millions of colors)—as well as from other platforms. Always keep in mind that color on the Web is highly imperfect; it relies heavily on the client hardware and video display.

SPEEDY HTML FILES

Antimony Software's Mizer optimizes HTML files for fast downloads by removing extra space and superfluous formatting.

Jaggies And Ghosting On Transparent Graphics

"How do I get rid of the fringe and jaggies around my transparent graphics?" is one of the most frequently asked questions among neophyte Web-graphics designers. The answer is to render your transparent GIF graphics on the same background on which they will be displayed in the Web page. By rendering on the same background, you can be assured that the graphic will blend smoothly (through anti-aliasing) into the background, as the word "CLEAN" does in this example. (The words "FRINGE & JAG" were rendered on a white background.)

If you render your graphic on a light background and then place it on a darker background in the Web page, you will end up with a ghostly, fringy, jaggy mess. Patterned backgrounds can be a bit problematic. You might want to try rendering the graphic on a solid color rather than on the background tile. If you decide to use this method, you probably should select the dominant color in the pattern as your background color.

Pages Are Too Wide

Wide pages—those designed with a set width higher than 600 pixels (or so)—are compromised when viewed on computers equipped with 640¥480 displays. The following example uses a fixed-width table: Notice how the rightmost column never appears in a narrow browser window.

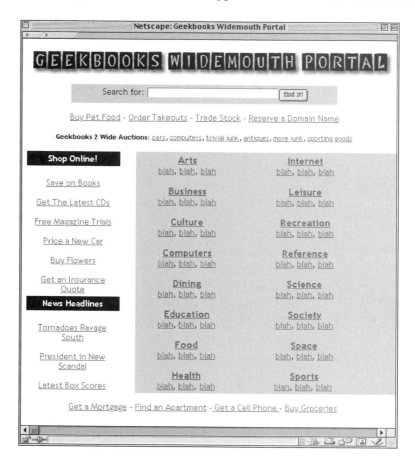

You can see an entire column hiding off to the right when you view it in a larger Web browser window. If you place your most important content there, visitors with lower-resolution monitors will never see it!

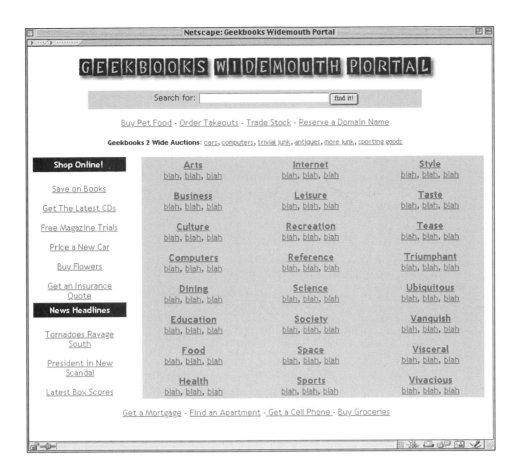

Many folks will miss that column; they won't bother to scroll horizontally. To avoid this situation, design with a 580- to 600-pixel maximum table layout, *or* use a table layout with a maximum width of 90 to 95 percent. Be a wise and gracious host. *Don't* tell your visitors that your site is best viewed with an 800-pixel (or wider) display.

Pages Are Too Long

Long pages can be cumbersome to view. Break up long pages into a series of shorter pages, while providing convenient navigation between all the pages, on each page. Breaking up pages facilitates faster downloading and display. You can place a linked table of contents on the first page and repeat the links at the bottom of each page.

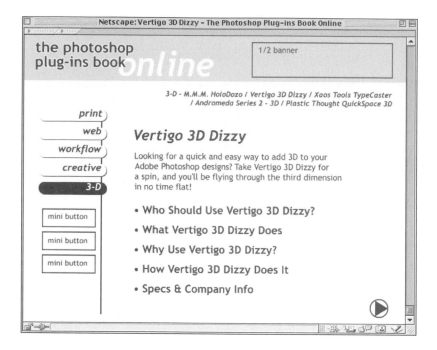

This practice poses a number of benefits, in addition to the faster downloads. These benefits include the following:

- *More advertising opportunities*—Each page allows for additional ad banner or button impressions.

- *More search engine listings*—The more pages on a subject, the more chances the site will have a strong showing.

- *Enhanced navigability*—Table of contents links allow visitors to quickly get to where they want to be.

Text Is Too Large (Or Too Small)

Having text with apparent font sizes that are too large is one of those thorny little cross-platform problems. When you specify the type size on a Macintosh, the type appears larger when viewed on a Windows-driven PC. Conversely, when you specify type size on a PC, the type appears smaller when viewed on a Macintosh. The following example shows the original page, as designed and viewed on a PC.

Now, here's the same PC example page, viewed on a Macintosh. Compare these two examples to see just how different a Web page can look.

It Looks Like A Circus

If your idea of a great Web experience is a page full of animated GIFs, hopping, jumping, spinning, and flashing like a three-ring extravaganza, consider running off and joining the circus rather than designing Web pages. Hey, it's a career choice!

The more your site feels like it belongs under the big top, the less seriously your visitors will consider it to be.

Advertising Overwhelms The Content

Which came first, the racecar or the sponsor's decal? If your pages primarily contain advertising banners and buttons, you have a problem. What's going to entice people to come to your site? What's going to make them want to come back? Advertising should defer to content. Fans tune in the race and come out to the track to see the cars and drivers racing, not to watch the commercials or see the decals.

Metaphors Cloud Meaning

Stay on target, and tell your visitors *exactly* what you mean. Don't get lost in a sea of whimsical metaphors and cutesy text.

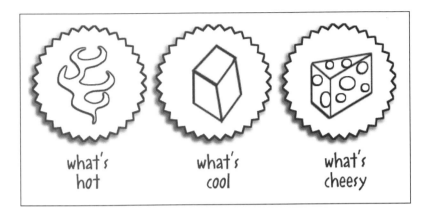

Poor Navigation

Although Chapter 7 is devoted to the topic of navigation, it deserves another mention here. Give your visitors the tools they need to find their way around your site. Keep your navigation design clean and simple. Provide a search function and a site map, as appropriate.

INSTANT SEARCH ENGINE!

Want to add a site search engine without CGI hassles? Check out the cool (free) search engine provided by Atomz.com.

Content Is Buried

Don't bury your most important content six levels down from your front page. For the best results, the crown jewels should never be more than two clicks away. If possible, make your page hierarchy short and wide rather than narrow and deep. The closer the most important content is to the top, the easier it will be to find, and the more likely it will be indexed by the search engines.

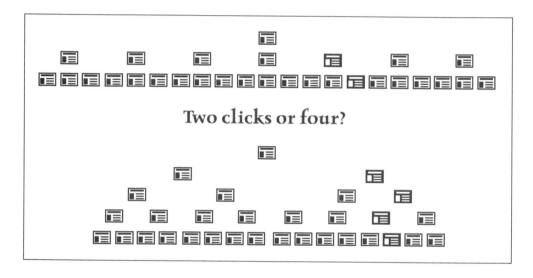

Two clicks or four?

It's Poorly Edited

Where have all the proofreaders gone? In the early eighties, I worked for a newspaper where the management decided that because it had put its writers and editors onto computer terminals, it didn't need all those curmudgeonly proofreaders. Guess what? It didn't work then, and it doesn't work now. Word-processor-based spelling and grammar checkers just don't cut it. The more human eyes you can put on a document, the better chance you have of catching errors *before* they're posted.

Of course, the Web offers a wonderful opportunity that the print world does not. If someone sees an error (typographical or otherwise) in a Web page, it's not a big issue to instantly fix the HTML page and repost it to the Web server. If an embarrassing error is found in the lead story of a metropolitan daily paper, the whole city will see it by lunchtime.

Poor Showing In The Search Engines

You'll have a tough time generating significant traffic if your site can't be found in the search engines and indexes. Make sure that your site shows up. Pay close attention to the following areas:

- *Page Titles*—These openers should be thorough yet concise. Try not to waste a single word. A well-written, carefully honed page title is essential for search engine success.

- *META Tags*—Use only relevant keywords and descriptions. Don't attempt to pull the wool over the search engines' eyes. The keywords and description should *accurately* describe the content of your site—no more, no less.

- *Descriptive Text*—If possible, the first text content on the page should provide a snapshot of what the page contains. Think of the first paragraph in a newspaper story. If you like what you read in the first paragraph, you'll read the story. If not, you'll ditch it and move on to the next.

Broken Links: It Goes 404

Have you ever traveled a long way to get to your destination only to find the lights darkened and the windows shuttered upon your arrival? Stay on top of your links. Don't let them go bad. Don't let your pages go 404. Avoid deleting or renaming pages without a provision to forward visitors to the new pages (or to replacement pages).

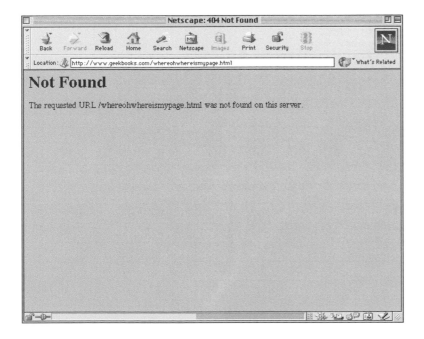

It Doesn't Sell

Whether for products or ideas, many Web sites exist to sell, sell, sell. If the pages are not moving products or propelling your ideas, you're bound to have a problem. A sales-oriented site should be continuously setting its mark. Traffic-generation campaigns must drive sufficient numbers of qualified visitors to the site. A system must exist to turn that traffic into leads and the leads into sales.

Nobody's Home

Commercial Web sites need all the credibility they can muster. When potential customers walk off the street into a bricks-and-mortar store, they know that the establishment actually exists. The potential customers can see the goods, soak in the ambiance, and consult with the staff. On the Web, this physical reassurance is lacking. In its place stands the strength of the brand; but the brand cannot stand alone. A commercial site should tell the visitors who you are, what you're about, where you're located, how to get in contact with you, and why you should earn their trust. Don't hide the truth. Let them know where you live.

It's Not Fresh

Have you ever seen a Web site so out of date that it's painful? Consider the Web merchant with the unfortunate practice of maintaining (or failing to maintain) an out-of-date, first-come-first-served clearance sale page. Unhappy customers attempt to purchase goods that have left the loading dock months earlier. How about the promotional page that trumpets an upcoming event, months or even years *after* the event has taken place. Disappointed visitors leave with an ambiguous feeling.

Keep your site fresh. Remove all out-of-date materials promptly. Update your time-sensitive pages frequently, and add a timestamp to show the most recent update.

It's A One-Way Street

The Web is a dynamic medium that provides for a high degree of interaction between the publisher and the reader. A Web site should not be a one-way street. People expect that, because it's *online*, it should be *instantaneous*. If you (as the publisher) do not acknowledge this assumed reality, you'll soon start losing your audience. As I was in the process of writing this book, I encountered a few incidents that illustrate this point:

- *I went looking for a new vacuum cleaner*. Our house has a 20-year-old built-in vacuum cleaning system that, for as long as we've lived here, has never worked all that well. It's due for a replacement. After finding a manufacturer of central vacuum-cleaner systems, I happily filled out its demographic form—which offered an exciting videotape and brochure—and waited for a follow-up email or phone call. After days of waiting (and no response), I started looking elsewhere.

Moral of the story: If you're going to use your Web site to gather leads, you should follow up on those leads immediately.

- *One of my computer monitors went on the fritz.* I went to the monitor manufacturer's Web site, found the support pages, and filled out the proper form and sent it off. I waited and waited for *any* kind of response from the form. After waiting a day or two for something to arrive, I gave up. Although the telephone customer service representative was wonderful, in the meantime I had to purchase another monitor to keep working. This company lost a repeat customer; the new monitor was from a different manufacturer.

  Moral of the story: If you're going to offer technical support via your Web site, do it right.

- *I placed an order with a Web merchant.* The merchant never sent an email acknowledging my order. I had no clue as to whether or not the merchant received the order. After a few days, I inquired to see whether the order had been shipped. I received a prompt response letting me know that a backordered item had held up shipment of the order and that it would ship that day.

  Moral of the story: If you are selling products over the Internet, provide an immediate order-confirmation email, as well as an email upon shipment. If an order is delayed, provide a status email.

Moving On

Web design has never been a do-it-once-and-forget-it affair. You're going to mess up at some point down the line. Don't kid yourself; *everyone* does. The information provided in this chapter should help you from straying off course. Responsible Web site design encompasses more than just cool graphics and layouts. It's enough to say that a Web designer's job is never done. If something doesn't work right, tweak it. If it's broken, fix it. The next chapter looks at challenges that you might encounter when you're ready to redesign your Web site.

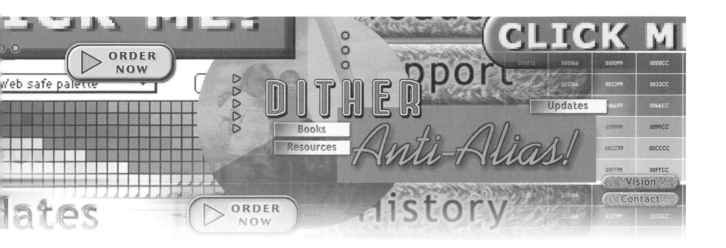

REDESIGN TIME

12

One thing's certain about Web site design: It's a never-ending task.

Rest assured. No sooner than your Web site is posted, you (and your clients) will start making changes. The Web's great that way: Typos can be fixed on the fly, rewrites can happen overnight, and pages can be tweaked and tuned at will. Full-bore Web site redesigns, however, are another matter. Redesigning a site can be a major undertaking that takes a lot of thought, planning, and testing.

Web site redesign is not a task to take lightly. Before you begin a redesign, start by asking one key question: What will the site do for your goals after the redesign that it's not doing now?

Prepare For Redesign

We've come full circle since Chapter 1. As a site is initially planned, the design process starts with theories and hypotheses. After a site has been active for some time, you have some data on which to prove (or disprove) those initial theories. This data can come in many forms, but it is most often found through the careful analysis of your Web server logs. It's also a good idea to store and categorize feedback received in the form of user emails.

The preparation for site redesign should include a number of key steps:

- Determine where the current site falls short.

- Identify those areas that can be improved without a total redesign of the site.

- Come up with two or more possible courses of action.

- Determine the amount of resources necessary to implement each course of action.

- Weigh the costs and benefits, choose a course, and get to work.

Design With Flexibility In Mind

If you've designed a flexible site, updating shouldn't be a painful procedure. You might be able to revise significant portions of the Web site by simply swapping out key components, such as background images, navigational graphics, and Cascading Style Sheets. These changes can make a dramatic difference in site appearance, without a huge amount of effort. You can make site-wide changes to navigational graphics and background images by executing a search-and-replace operation on all the HTML files. Powerful text editors, such as BBEdit, make this procedure a snap. Most Web site-creation programs should include site-wide search-and-replace capabilities as well. Although the specifications for

BACK UP FIRST!

Make a complete backup of your live site *before* you start the redesign process. Put this backup in a safe place, just in case.

Cascading Style Sheets are not finalized and some Web browsers either do not support or only partially support this feature, you can learn more about compatibility issues at **http://webreview.com/wr/pub/guides/style/mastergrid.html**.

Implementing major changes to page or site structure can be much more difficult. This subject is covered in the following two sections.

Decide What Stays And What Goes

After you've dug through your statistics, you'll know which pages are popular and which are not. Don't be rash and dump all of your low-traffic pages. Be selective in the pages you prune.

In general, you should throw out pages that you find will fall into either one or both of the following categories:

- Pages that support products or initiatives that are no longer part of the grand scheme

- Pages that herald an upcoming event, long after the event has passed

Search And Destroy

You should remove a lot of the little irritating design elements upon redesign. Take this duty as an opportunity to clean up your act. You will want to avoid or eliminate the following features:

- *Table borders*—Most tables can live without borders. In many cases, the design will be better served with variations in row or column color rather than with a gawky table border.

- *Frame borders*—In the early days of frames, all framed layouts also had borders. As the Web browsers evolved, the developers added the capability to create nonbordered framesets. If you have a framed Web site that uses borders between the frames, it's time for your site to evolve as well.

- *Blinking text*—Need I say more?

Behind The Curtains

Don't perform your magic while in the public eye. As you prepare your revised Web site, you should work behind the curtains—just like that man at the end of *The Wizard of Oz*. Folks don't want to see your site until it's ready for prime time. Avoid working on the publicly accessed version of your site. Instead, work on a privately posted version. Make all the changes *before* you cut in the new site. Only after you are completely satisfied that everything on your pages—image maps, icons, graphics, hyperlink text, forms, and so on—works, should you put your site where the world will see it.

Cut In The New Site

After you have thoroughly tested and okayed the Web site on a private Web server, you should move all the updated pages over to the public Web server. Obviously, you don't want to make this move during a busy period. Study your server statistics, and pick a quiet time to FTP the entire site. As soon as you move all the files over to the live server, begin testing immediately. Have a team of volunteers tear through the (now) public site, checking every link. Fix any broken links that you find, FTP the revised pages, and continue testing.

Many things can break when you move files from one server to the next. So that you can avoid tons of broken links (both hyperlinks and inline graphics), it's essential that you make the file directory structure on the private testing server follow the exact same file directory structure that will be on the public server. Renaming files and directories can be a dicey procedure.

Prevent 404 Errors

The infamous "Page Not Found-404" errors, as mentioned in the preceding chapter, are the bane of site redesigns. It pays to be diligent to avoid 404s. Good Web site-management software can help you find and fix any broken links. When automated link-checking first appeared in standalone programs such as Adobe SiteMill (now discontinued), Webmasters happily paid hundreds of dollars for the functionality. These days, the very same features are available in inexpensive Web site-creation applications. Adobe PageMill, for example, includes all of the Web site-management tools once found in SiteMill. Double-check all links, and replace all of the pages you deleted with forwarding pages.

Web Page Examples

The following sections provide a number of examples of Web page redesigns and concepts. These examples focus on practical applications, and although most are just make-believe representations for illustrative use, they represent both good and poor Web page design.

NIX THE CONSTRUCTION SIGNS

Don't even think about using an "Under Construction" graphic. *Every* site is under construction. Those signs aren't cute, and they're not constructive. They're just pointless, and they could hint that you lack a fully developed plan for the site.

DON'T OVERLOOK THE META TAGS

Make sure that the revised pages have the proper META tags before posting them to the public server.

The Kite Shop

Every small shop owner should think about how the Internet affects his or her business. This example uses an imaginary kite shop, Allycat's Waycool Kites, which I developed for this chapter. The original home page is very basic, with just a drop-shadowed photograph for embellishment. Although this page gets the point across in an unfettered manner, it lacks punch.

The updated home page is bold and colorful, with a large, playful cloud background and bright kite graphics. The images make use of a limited palette of flat, Web browser-safe colors. The navigational graphics use JavaScript rollovers, with a large area at the bottom right that provides room for details on each selection. In all, the revamped design delivers a lot of color and information with a respectable (i.e., a relatively quick) download time for your visitors.

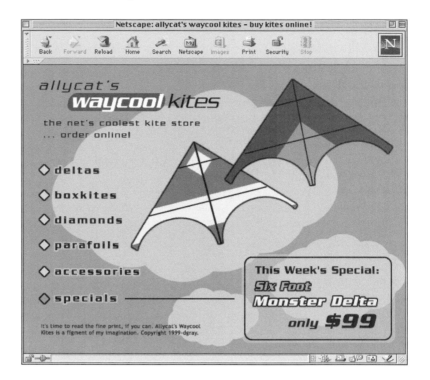

The Car For Sale

The Internet provides a wonderful marketplace for collector automobiles. Unfortunately, many sellers treat the medium as they would a newspaper classified advertisement. Your advertisement has so much more potential on the Web! With a conventional printed classified ad, you would most likely have a text-only advertisement. Although some specialized publications offer black-and-white or even color photos, these niceties can be expensive, and the resulting printed images tend to be coarse and grainy when they appear on inexpensive paper or newsprint.

Although the text in the following make-believe classified listing may be compelling, the Royal Bobcat GTO still has a rough time leaping out at the reader and capturing his or her imagination.

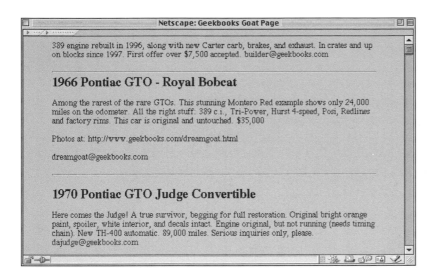

This next example repeats the same text used in the classified, but the full-color photograph tells a much better story. The photo clears up the question of "What does Montero Red look like?" as the rims shine and the Tri-Power carburetors sparkle from underneath the hood. The link to photos provides the opportunity to include far more than just a JPEG. What could be cooler than including a sound file of that 389 motor rumbling through the dual exhaust or perhaps a QuickTime movie of the GTO in action? Talk about baiting the hook!

The Auction Page

Internet auction mania has swept the globe. Everyone wants to buy or sell something online—from Beanie Babies to antique collectibles—in the world's largest flea market. There's no limit to what folks will auction off online.

Let's say you have some extra tickets to the hottest rock and roll show of the summer. If you put a simple auction listing on eBay (or another auction site), what kind of bidding would you expect?

> **Springsteen Tickets** - The Meadowlands - Wednesday August 4th, 1999. We ended up with 4 extra awesome stageside seats. They could be yours. Section 112, Row 13 (first level). No obstructions. bruuuuuce@geekbooks.com

A graphic auction listing informs potential bidders and inspires confidence by displaying a scanned image of the actual tickets, along with a simple diagram that shows the seat location, relative to the stage. It's always a good idea to check the laws before you post any ticket auctions, to ensure that you're not violating ticket-scalping regulations. (FYI, I didn't sell these tickets. It was an amazing show!)

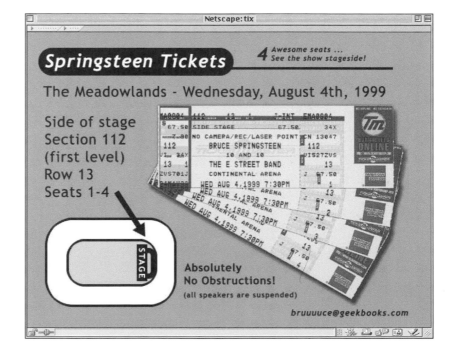

The Photoshop Plug-ins Book

The following Web page is an actual example of a book being revised into a Web site. I wrote *The Photoshop Plug-ins Book* for Ventana Press in 1997, with the understanding that the book would be updated on an annual basis. Unfortunately, Ventana closed its doors shortly after the book was published, and the book was never revised. Although the book remained in print until mid-1999, I began planning a Web site to pick up where the book left off. Commitments kept me away from the project, although I fell asleep many nights, dreaming of a site that would provide an ongoing virtual encyclopedia of Photoshop plug-ins.

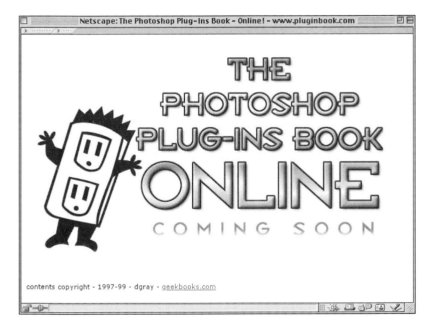

The Photoshop Plug-ins Book Online (**http://pluginsbook.com**) is very much a work in process. Its final form will likely look different than the example shown here.

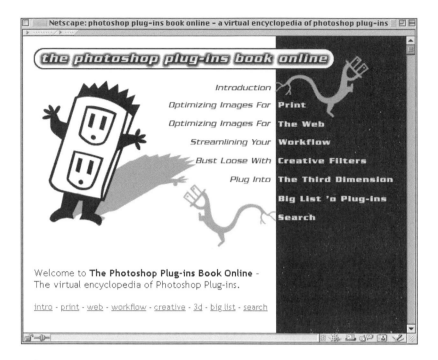

Moving On

Web site design is a continuous, evolutionary process with many opportunities for corrections to course. This chapter covered just a handful of the issues that you may encounter when redesigning a site. The "Resources" appendix and Glossary that follow this chapter were designed to provide you with reference material and links that will come in handy as you get fully underway in the world of Web design.

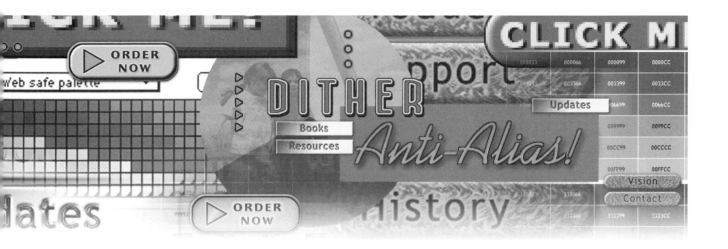

APPENDIX
RESOURCES

Do you need more information on a specific topic or some cool downloadable goodies? Look no further! This appendix provides listings of Internet resources related to Web design. You'll find a host of JavaScript, CGI, animation, clip art, font, advertising and market data sites, and more.

JavaScript and DHTML—add interactivity to your pages.

Web Site	Address
Builder.com SuperScripter	http://www.builder.com/Programming/Kahn/
Developer.com JavaScript Directory	http://www.developer.com/directories/pages/dir.javascript.html
Dynamic Drive	http://dynamicdrive.com
Java Goodies	http://www.javagoodies.com
JavaScripts.com	http://www.javascripts.com
JavaScript Source	http://javascript.internet.com
JavaScript World	http://www.jsworld.com
Nic's JavaScript Page	http://www.geocities.com/~jsmaster
WebCoder.com	http://www.webcoder.com
Website Abstraction	http://wsabstract.com

CGI scripts—put some smarts on your server.

Web Site	Address
BigNoseBird.com	http://www.bignosebird.com
The CGI Resource Index	http://www.cgi-resources.co
Click-Scripts CGI Archive	http://www.staff.net/cgi-scripts
Response-O-Matic	http://www.response-o-matic.com
ScriptsSearch	http://www.scriptsearch.com

GIF animation and clip art—need some art fast? Check out these sites.

Web Site	Address
A-1 Icon Archive	http://www.free-graphics.com
Andy's Art Attack	http://www.andyart.com
Animation City	http://www.animationcity.net
ArtToday	http://www.arttoday.com
Caboodles!	http://www.caboodles.com
Clipart.com	http://www.clipart.com
Digit Mania	http://www.digitmania.holowww.com
Gifart.com	http://www.gifart.com
IconBAZAAR	http://www.iconbazaar.com
netCREATORS Icon Page	http://animatedgifs.simplenet.com
Online Logo Generator	http://www.cooltext.com
SSAnimation	http://ssanimation.com
Web GraFX-FX	http://www.webgrafx-fx.com

Fonts—search for freeware, shareware, and commercial-quality fonts.

Web Site	Address
007Fonts	http://www.007fonts.com
ArtToday	http://www.arttoday.com
Chris MacGregor's Internet Type Foundry Index	http://www.typeindex.com
DsgnHaus	http://www.fonthaus.com
EyeWire	http://www.eyewire.com
The Fontpool	http://www.fontpool.com
FontShop	http://www.fontshop.com
International Typeface Corporation	http://www.itcfonts.com
Phil's Fonts	http://www.philsfonts.com

Animated GIF builders—create your own cool animations.

Web Site	Address
Fireworks	http://www.macromedia.com
GIF Animator	http://www.ulead.com
GifBuilder	http://iawww.epfl.ch/Staff/Yves.Piguet/clip2gif-home/GifBuilder.html
GIF Movie Gear	http://www.coffeecup.com
GifDANCER	http://www.paceworks.com
GIFmation	http://www.boxtopsoft.com
ImageReady	http://www.adobe.com
Photo Cell	http://www.secondglance.com
Universal Animator	http://www.autofx.com
WebPainter	http://www.totallyhip.com

Java applet builders and customizable applets—pour some hot Java into your site.

Web Site	Address
1st JAVANavigator	http://www.auscomp.com
Chris Cobb's "Obligatory" Applets	http://www.ccobb.org
EarthWeb's JARS.COM	http://www.jars.com
electric butterfly online	http://www.ebutterfly.com
Formula Graphics	http://www.formulagraphics.com
FreeCode	http://www.freecode.com
IMC ActionLine	http://www.imcinfo.com
Mainstay PageCharmer	http://www.mstay.com/target.html
Modern Minds	http://www.modernminds.com
PaceWorks ObjectDANCER	http://www.paceworks.com
PageCharmer and PageMover	http://www.pagecharmer.com
PineappleSoft	http://www.pineapplesoft.com
The Java Boutique	http://javaboutique.internet.com
WebBurst and WebBurst FX	http://www.powerproduction.com
Webmonkey: Java Collection	http://www.hotwired.com/webmonkey/java

Shockwave—zap your site with 10,000 volts.

Web Site	Address
Ezone Tremors	http://www.ezone.com/tremors
Macromedia ShockRave	http://www.shockrave.com
Pop Rocket's Game Arena	http://www.poprocket.com/shockwave
@dver@ctive's Shock-Bauble Showcase	http://www.adveract.com

Sound and music—add some ambient music or playful sounds.

Web Site	Address
Classical MIDI Archives	http://prs.net/midi.html
Digital Kitchen	http://www.dkitchen.com
ifni MIDI archive	http://www.ifni.com/midi
MIDI Farm	http://www.midifarm.com/files
MIDI Jazz Network	http://miso.wwa.com/~blewis
MIDIWORLD	http://midiworld.com
Res Rocket	http://www.resrocket.com
Sampleheads	http://www.sampleheads.com
The Daily .WAV	http://www.dailywav.com
The Ultra-Lounge	http://www.ultralounge.com
Woo-hoo! It's Homer!	http://home.eznet.net/~davlin/homer.htm

Syndicated content—add some professional content to your site.

Web Site	Address
ISyndicate.com	http://www.isyndicate.com

Web site tracking—keep on eye on your Web site statistics.

Web Site	Address
eXTReMe Tracking	http://www.extreme-dm.com/tracking
HitBOX	http://www.hitbox.com

Web site hosts—find a ISP host for your site.

Web Site	Address
HostIndex.com Web Hosting Directory	http://www.hostindex.com

Affiliate program administrators—make your site pay its freight.

Web Site	Address
Be Free	http://www.befree.com
ClickTrade	http://www.clicktrade.com
Commission Junction	http://www.cj.com
Linkshare	http://www.linkshare.com

Advertising—build an advertising campaign.

Web Site	Address
24/7 Media	http://www.247media.com
DoubleClick	http://www.doubleclick.com
ValueClick	http://www.valueclick.com

Internet statistics and market research—get the skinny on who's going where and why.

Web Site	Address
Forrester Research	http://www.forrester.com
Jupiter Communications	http://www.jup.com
Media Metrix	http://www.mediametrix.com
StatMarket	http://www.statmarket.com

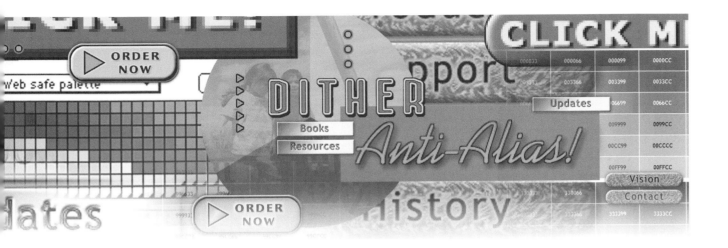

GLOSSARY

Add-on—A program that runs either inside or outside your Web browser. Add-ons perform a specialized task or handle a specific type of data. Chapter 9.

Address—See *URL*. Chapter 1.

Applet—A small application transmitted from a Web site to run on your computer. Java applications that download from an Internet server are examples of applets. Chapter 9.

Archive—A Web site that contains useful information, code, graphics, and so on. Also, a file that can contain many files, usually in compressed form. ZIP (PC) and StuffIt (Mac) are the most common file formats. Chapter 1.

Background image—The graphics file (often, a pattern file that is tiled) that you place on a Web page, which appears behind the text and graphic elements when a surfer accesses that page. Chapter 6.

Bandwidth—The size of the data pipe. The wider the bandwidth, the more data that can be pumped down from the server to the client. Dial-up connections with conventional (28.8 and 56K) modems are narrow bandwidth. Cable modems, DSL lines, and satellite connections provide broadband connections. Chapter 10.

Banner ad—The most common form of Internet advertising. Depending on the type of ad, the banner size used is usually a selection of one of five sizes. Chapters 1 and 10.

Bit—The smallest element of computer data. A bit is either a binary 1 or a binary 0 (zero).

Bitmapped graphic—A pixel-based graphic (editable in Photoshop and PaintShop Pro) that is generated by turning on and/or altering the intensity and color of specific screen elements called *pixels*. Chapter 2.

BMP—Bitmapped graphics. A PC image format. Chapter 2.

Browser—A program whose functions include navigating the World Wide Web, loading and displaying HTML documents and graphics, and handling associated tasks. (Also known as a Web browser.) Chapter 1.

Browser side—Occurring, taking place, or running on a user's Web browser program. Also, see *Client side*. Chapter 6.

Byte—A computer data character; it is composed of either 7 or 8 *bits*.

Cable modem—A modem that operates over cable TV lines. Because the coaxial cable used by cable TV provides much greater bandwidth than telephone lines, a cable modem can achieve fast access to the Web. With a single direction cable modem, you still need to be connected to a telephone line. Chapter 1.

Cascading Style Sheet (CSS)—A recently added feature to HTML that gives both Web site developers and users greater control over how pages display on various computers and operating systems. Web designers and users can create style sheets that define how elements such as headers, fonts, and links are displayed. Because the specification is still evolving, it may not be fully supported by your Web browser. Chapter 12.

CGI—Acronym for Common Gateway Interface. CGI acts as an interface between Web pages and programs running on a host machine, funneling information between the program and the Web page. Chapter 3.

Character style—A physical HTML tag that performs formatting changes on characters, words, or phrases within a paragraph. Character styles include *Italics* and **boldface**. Chapter 2.

Click-through—An Internet advertising term: A visitor clicks on a Web ad (most often a banner) and goes to the advertiser's Web site. The advertiser's cost of placing this ad on another's Web site is often determined either by the number of times it's viewed and/or viewed and used. Chapter 10.

Clickable image—A graphic image that is also designed to be a hyperlink. An image that contains multiple hyperlinks is called an *image map*. Chapter 7.

Client—An application that performs a function on behalf of another application. For example, WS_FTP (Windows) and Fetch (Mac) are FTP clients. Chapter 6.

Client side—Occurring, taking place, or running on an enduser's application. Also, see *browser side*. Chapter 6.

Contextual graphic—An electronic file of art and photographs that are carefully chosen to thoroughly integrate with the Web page text they are supposed to illuminate. Good contextual graphics, when present, add value to the total text. Poorly chosen graphics detract from the text. Chapter 5.

DHTML—Dynamic HTML. Dynamic HTML documents, the components of DHTML pages, are HTML, JavaScript, and Cascading Style Sheets. First found in the version 4 Web browsers, DHTML allows JavaScript to take charge of *Document Object Model (DOM)* elements. Chapter 9.

Dingbat—A tiny picture, such as a star, checkmark, or pointing hand that you can insert into a document. In the publishing world, dingbats are often used as bullet list illustrations or to signify the end of an article or chapter. In the computer world, dingbats are available as fonts. Zapf Dingbats is the most popular dingbat font. Chapter 5.

Document—On the Web, an HTML *page*. Less often, an image or program file associated with an HTML page. Chapter 1.

DOM (Document Object Model)—A specification for how Web-page objects (text, images, headers, links, and so on) are displayed. DOM defines the attributes that are associated with each object and how you can manipulate these objects and attributes. *DHTML* relies on the DOM to dynamically alter the look of Web pages after they download to a user's Web browser. Chapter 9.

Domain name—An Internet name that identifies one or more IP addresses. For example, the domain name **coriolis.com** may represent more than one IP address. Domain names are used in URLs to identify Web pages. Chapter 1.

DSL (Digital Subscriber Line)—A type of modem line that allows for a fast broadband connection to the Internet, operating at speeds up to 1.5Mbps. DSL lines can carry voice, fax, and data simultaneously.

eCommerce—Web-based selling of a product or service. Chapter 1.

FAQ—A list of Frequently Asked Questions on a given subject, along with answers. FAQs are a common means of providing information needed by those new to the Internet. Chapter 1.

Form—A client-side Web document that contains blank fields in which users enter data. On the Web, the HTML language uses codes to display form elements such as text fields, radio buttons, and checkboxes. A server-side CGI application processes the data entered into a Web-based form. JavaScript also may act upon the data. Chapter 3.

Frame—A Web design scheme that allows the designer to create a single Web page from multiple HTML files. The final result is an apparently single page, broken into two or more boxes, with each box functioning as an individual "section" of the page. The framset surrounds and contains these box sections. Chapter 7.

Freeware—Software that is distributed free of charge. Chapter 9.

FTP (File Transfer Protocol)—A protocol that enables file transfer over the Internet.

Gamma correction—A software-based system adjustment made to affect the brightness of the monitor. Usually, gamma correction software is either built into high-level applications, or a separate application is provided. Chapter 4.

GIF (Graphics Interchange Format)—An indexed-color format graphic, originally popularized on CompuServe. GIF is one of the two most common graphic image formats on the Web. (The other format is *JPEG.*) Chapter 5.

Home page—Strictly speaking, the first or index page on a Web site. *Home page* is often used to refer to a *Web site.* A home page is the first HTML document you see when you go to a Web site. Chapter 1.

Host—A computer connected directly to the Internet (unlike a Web surfer, who connects indirectly through an Internet service provider's server), usually one that acts as a server for Web pages. See also *Server.* Chapters 1 and 3.

HTML (Hypertext Markup Language)—A relatively simple language consisting of *tags* in text documents that produce special text effects and formatting (fonts, boldface, and so on) to generate Web pages. HTML tags also call graphics and other documents for display, among other functions. Chapter 2.

http (Hypertext transfer protocol)—The prefix of the *URL* for every page on the Web. This address prefix is an Internet protocol that tells a Web browser to look for an HTML document or other file on the Web (as opposed to on its computer's disk drive).

Hyperlink—Within an HTML document, a clickable link to another document or to a different portion of the same document. Chapter 2.

Hypertext—A document (or segment thereof) that contains links to other documents; another name for an HTML document. Chapter 9.

Icons—Small pictures, usually representing an object or program. Icons are a principal feature of graphical user interface design and—if carefully chosen or created—are a popular way to add easy-to-understand visual links on Web pages. Chapter 5.

Image map—A clickable graphic image on a Web page that is divided into zones or regions, and each zone is linked to a different URL, image, or other object. Chapter 7.

Index page—See *Home page.* Chapter 8.

Inline graphic—An image displayed by a Web page. Chapters 2 and 6.

InterNIC— A project of AT&T and Network Solutions, Inc., InterNIC is supported by the National Science Foundation. Among other services, the project currently offers registration services and lookup capabilities for domain names and IP addresses. Chapter 1.

Interstitial—An advertisement or other promotional piece that appears in between content pages. Chapter 10.

IP address (Internet Protocol address)—A numeric 32-bit address that contains information necessary to identify a specific network and machine on the Internet. Chapter 1.

ISDN (Integrated Services Digital Network)—A type of modem line that allows for continuous connection to the Internet, at speeds up to 128K. ISDN lines can carry voice, fax, and data simultaneously. Chapter 11.

ISP (Internet Service Provider)—A company that provides connection to the Internet. An ISP may be a consumer online service (such as CompuServe or America Online) or an independent service provider. Usually, however, the term refers to independent ISPs. Chapter 3.

Java—A specialized, cross-platform programming language that can be used with Web pages. A Java program is an *applet* that is transmitted to and run on a computer that requests its Web page. Chapters 3 and 9.

JavaScript—A scripting language that can be used to incorporate interactivity into a Web page. JavaScript is particularly useful because it can interact with HTML source code and user input. Chapters 3 and 9.

JPEG—A graphic image format created by the Joint Photo Experts Group. JPEG is a popular graphics format on the Web because its file size can be reduced—if done with care—without sacrificing apparent image quality. Chapter 4.

Link—On a Web page, a link is a hypertext reference to another document, either on the same Web site or on another site altogether. Chapters 1 and 2.

META tag—A special HTML tag that gives information about a Web page. Unlike standard HTML, META tags do not affect how the page is displayed; they provide data such as the page's creator, its update schedule, the page's description, and which keywords represent the page's content. Many search engines employ this data to build their databases. Chapters 1 and 7.

Modem—An acronym for "MOdulator/DEModulator," a modem is a device or program that enables a computer to transmit data over telephone lines. Chapter 1.

Network—A group of multiple computers, interlinked and sharing resources. In the narrowest sense, two interlinked computers make up a network. In the broadest sense, the Internet is a network.

Notepad—A simple Windows-based text editor. Chapter 1.

Online service—A dial-up commercial computer service that exists independent of the Internet but may be connected to the Internet. The most popular online services that also serve as ISPs are America Online, CompuServe, and The Microsoft Network. Chapter 6.

Ornamental graphic—An image added to a Web page to convey a mood or to add visual interest to the page. Chapter 5.

Page—Collectively, an HTML document and its supporting files (images, text, JavaScript, and so on). Also, see *Web page*. Chapter 1.

Paragraph format—A style used by HTML to make specific changes to an entire block of text, up to the line break. Examples of paragraph formats are heading formats, body text formats, and list formats. Chapter 2.

Pixel—Short for picture element. The smallest element of an image on a display device. Chapter 4.

Plug-in—A program added to your Web browser to expand or enhance its capabilities. A Web browser runs the plug-in to handle a specific type of data transmitted by a Web page. Chapter 2.

Resolution—On a display device, the relative quality of a graphic image, based on its density (the number of pixels used). The higher the resolution, the greater amount of information displayed. The most common display resolutions are 640×480, 800×600, and 1024×768. Chapter 5.

Revenue sharing—An Internet advertising method by which both the advertiser and the Web site owner who accept the advertiser's banner share a percentage of the profits of a successful ad campaign. This method is often referred to as *associate* or *affiliate marketing*. Chapter 10.

RGB (red, green, blue)—The additive process used by computer monitors to display, in pixels, text and images. Chapter 4.

Sans serif—A simple, unadorned font design that doesn't include fiddley bits such as the curly "bump" at the top of the letter *f*. An example of a sans-serif font is Helvetica. Chapter 2.

Script language—A simple programming language with which you can write scripts. Perl (which runs at the server) and JavaScript (which runs at the browser) are examples of script languages. Chapters 3 and 9.

Search engine—A program that searches a database containing information about millions of Web pages. When queried for information, the search engine presents a list of Web pages that meet the query's search criteria. Chapters 1 and 7.

Search facility—A program that's similar to a *search engine*, but all searches occur within the "boundaries" of a single Web site or of a particular cluster of related sites. Chapter 8.

Serif—A font that is more ornate than simple, and includes additions such as decorations on the upper-right and lower-left ends of the letter *S*. An example of a serif font is Times Roman. Chapter 2.

Server—A computer that provides resources to other computers. On the Internet, a server is usually any host for HTML documents and other files that are available to other computers. Also, the computer on which a given set of resources (such as the pages that make up a Web site) is stored and which—upon your browser's request—sends you HTML documents. Chapter 3.

Server side—Occurring, taking place, or running on a Web server. Chapter 3.

Shareware—Software that is distributed on a try-before-you-buy basis. Chapter 9.

SimpleText—A simple Macintosh-based text editor. Chapter 1.

Site—See *Web site*.

Site map—An area (often, a separate Web page) that contains methods (usually, hypertext links) that users can use to more easily find their way around a Web site that has many pages. A link to the site map is generally placed at the same location (either top, side, or bottom) of every page on the site. Chapter 8.

Splash page—The initial screen serves as an introduction to the site; often referred to as the *home page*. Chapter 8.

Sponsored content—Web pages (or complete Web sites) whose creators are compensated in a similar manner as that which a company might sponsor a sporting or cultural event. The sponsor pays for the development of content instead of purchasing advertising space. Chapter 10.

Streaming media—A data-transfer technique that processes information as a steady, continuous stream. The most-common streamed data on the Internet is currently audio and video files. Because most users lack the access speed to download large multimedia files quickly, streaming can help a client browser or plug-in start displaying the information before the entire file is transmitted. RealAudio and QuickTime are examples of streaming media applications. Chapter 9.

Tags—The codes used in HTML documents that indicate text is to be used as special elements, such as lists, heads, hypertext, and so on. HTML tags are enclosed in greater-than/less-than symbols < >. Chapter 2.

URL (Uniform Resource Locator)—A Web-address name, such as **www.coriolis.com**, that you use to navigate to a specific Web site or page, and to identify a specific Web page. Chapter 1.

Web—Short for the World Wide Web. Sometimes called the WWW or (incorrectly) "the Net," the Web is a globe-spanning hypertext network consisting of tens of millions of Web pages. The Web is the graphical portion of the Internet. Chapter 1.

Web page—See *Page*.

Web site—A specific set of related and interconnected documents made up of HTML code, graphics, and supporting applications hosted on a computer that is connected to the Internet. Collectively, these documents are referred to as a Web site. Chapter 1.

WYSIWYG—An acronym for "What you see is what you get" (a term borrowed from comedian Flip Wilson). This term implies that an application is capable of producing screen-accurate output (the text will appear in the final viewed version—whether on screen, on paper, or in some other form—just as it appears in the application that created it).

INDEX

COLOPHON

From start to finish, The Coriolis Group designed *Looking Good On The Web* with the creative professional in mind.

The cover was produced on a Power Macintosh using QuarkXPress 3.3 for layout compositing. Text imported from Microsoft Word was restyled using the Futura and Trajan font families from the Adobe font library. It was printed using four-color process and spot UV coating.

Select images from the color chapter were combined with new images to form the color montage art strip, unique for each Creative Professionals Press book.

The color chapter was assembled using Adobe Pagemaker 6.5 on a G3 Macintosh system. Images in TIFF format were color corrected and sized in Adobe Photoshop 5. It was printed using four-color process.

The interior layout was built in Adobe Pagemaker 6.5 on a Power Macintosh. Adobe fonts used include Stone Informal for body, Avenir Black for heads, and Copperplate 31ab for chapter titles. Adobe Photoshop 4 was used to process grayscale. Text originated in Microsoft Word.

Imagesetting and manufacturing were completed by Courier, Stoughton, Ma.

If you like this book, you'll love these...

FLASH 4 WEB ANIMATION F/X AND DESIGN

Ken Milburn and John Croteau
ISBN: 1-57610-555-5 • $49.99
500 pages with CD-ROM

Build compelling Web sites utilizing the newest features of Flash 4. Case studies illustrate the successful implementation of Flash animation on actual Web sites, which you can learn and then use for your own sites. *Flash 4 f/x and design* enhances the material found in the previous edition, *Flash 3 f/x and design*, by adding new information on advanced animation techniques, such as transparency, Flash movies, exporting to other formats, and Action Scripts.

ADOBE IMAGESTYLER IN DEPTH

Daniel Gray
ISBN: 1-57610-410-9 • $39.99
400 pages with CD-ROM

Stop pushing those pixels around and supercharge your Web graphics with Adobe ImageStyler! You'll learn the ins and outs of ImageStyler in an easy-to-read, hands-on manner. *Adobe ImageStyler In Depth* dives into the program's features and goes far beyond the program's documentation to help you take your designs to the next level.

ADOBE PAGEMILL 3 F/X AND DESIGN

Daniel Gray
ISBN: 1-57610-214-9 • $39.99
250 pages with CD-ROM

Adobe PageMill 3 f/x and design puts you in the driver's seat by providing all the tools you'll need to create beautiful, functional Web sites. Hands-on tutorials quickly get you behind the wheel and on your way to Web success. Best-selling author, Daniel Gray, tears off the shrinkwrap and goes beyond the box—delivering information in an easy-to-read and informative manner.

LOOKING GOOD IN PRINT

Roger C. Parker
ISBN: 1-56604-856-7 • $29.99
280 pages

The most widely used design companion for desktop publishers, *Looking Good In Print* gives you the guidance you need. You'll learn the basic elements of design—typography, basic accents, illustrations, photographs, and color—to achieve the special effects you want. Then, you'll apply your newfound knowledge to creating specific documents, such as newsletters, advertisements, brochures, and whatever else you desire.

The Coriolis Group, LLC   Telephone: 1.800.410.0192 • www.coriolis.com
Coriolis books are also available at bookstores and computer stores nationwide.